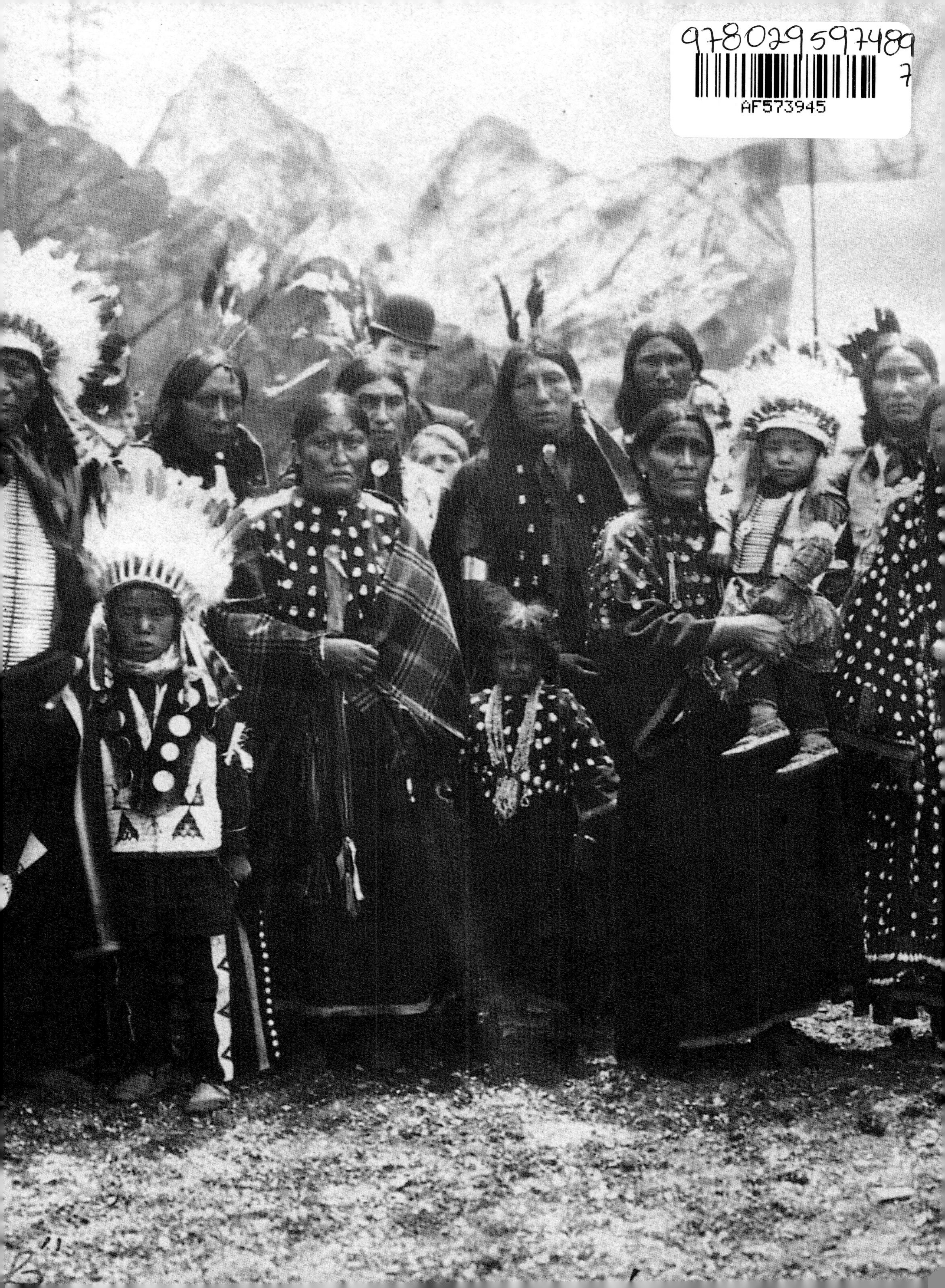

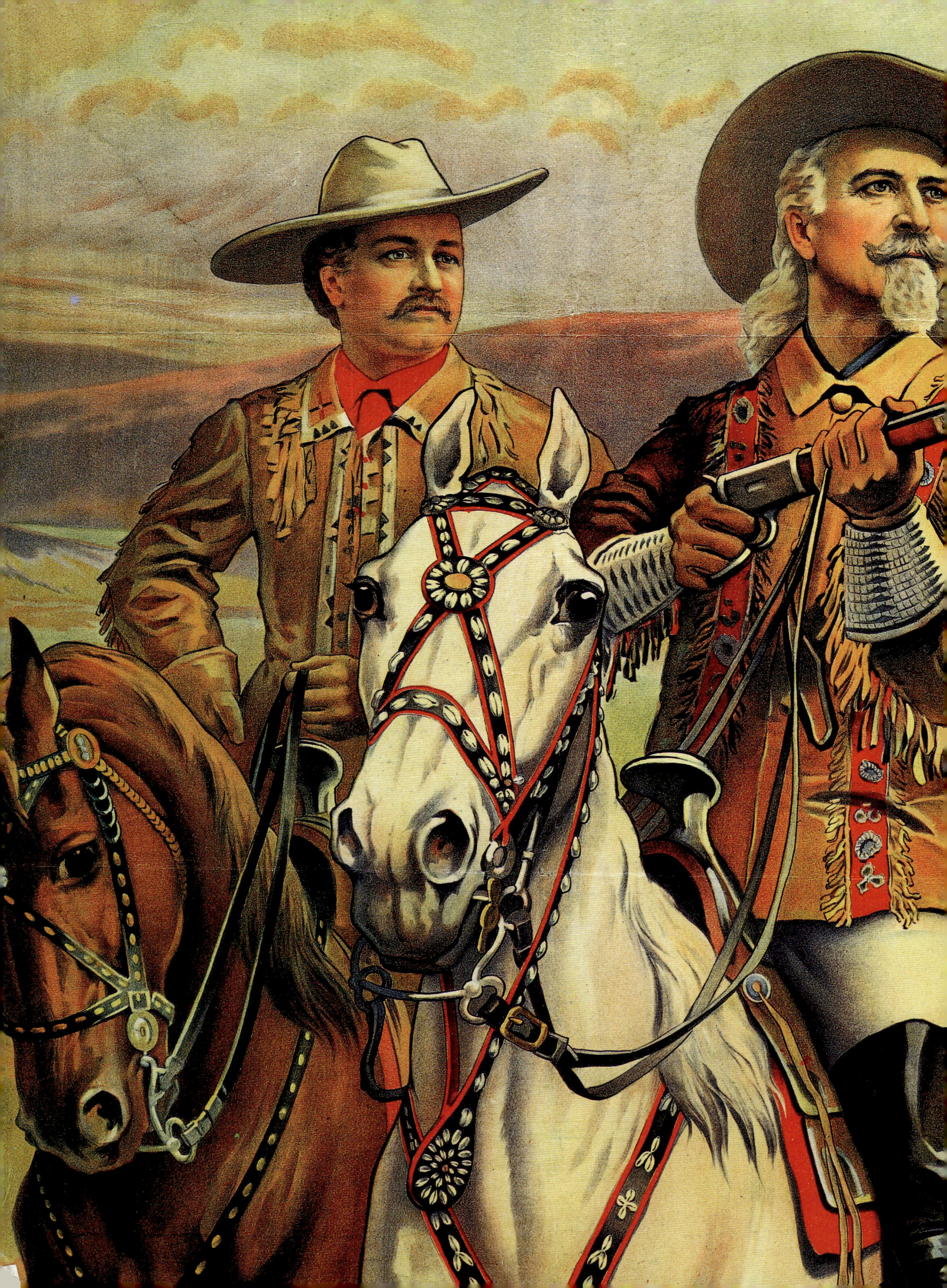

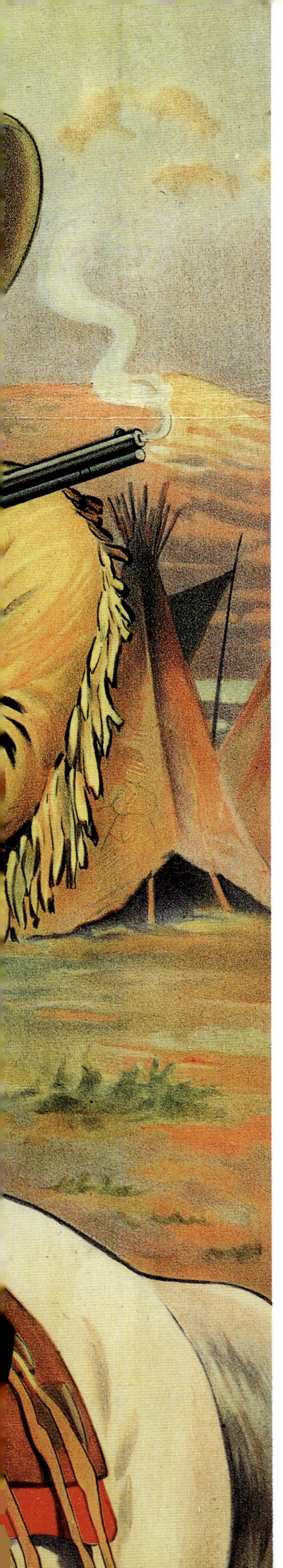

Buffalo Bill Historical Center • Cody, Wyoming

Buffalo Bill Museum

Table of Contents

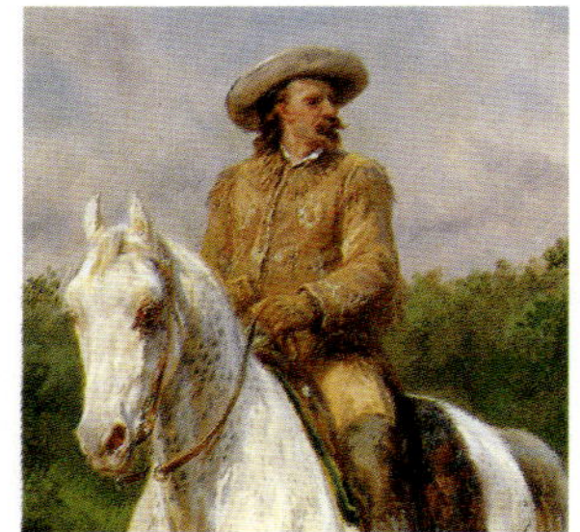

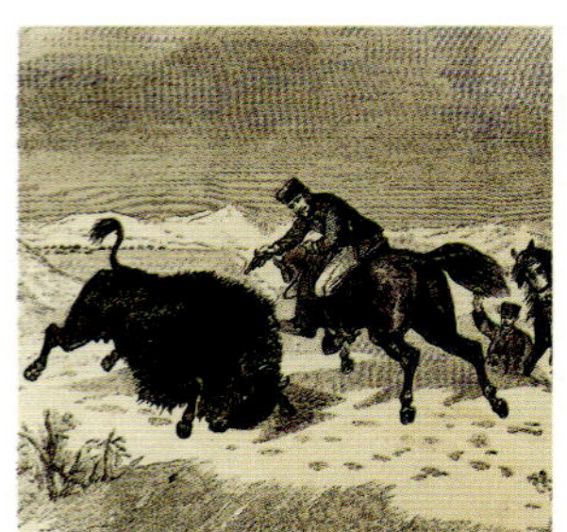

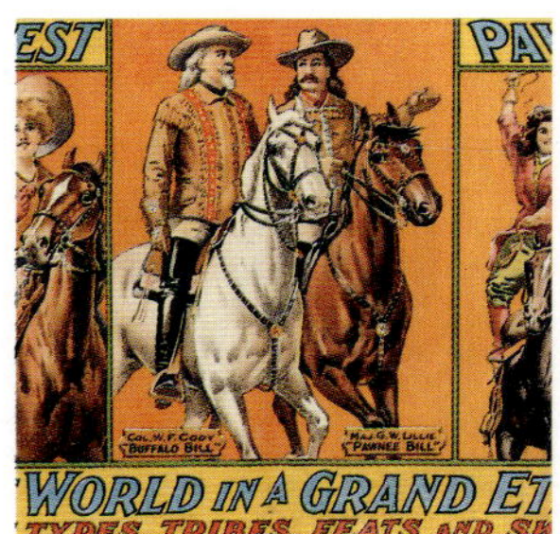

Following Page:
The Pulp Industry:
New York Weekly,
Vol. XXVII, No. 20,
March 25, 1872.
(Detail)

Previous Page:
The Two Bills, c.1912.
U.S. Lithograph Co.,
Russel-Morgan Print.
Lithograph; 39 1/2 in. x 27 1/2 in.

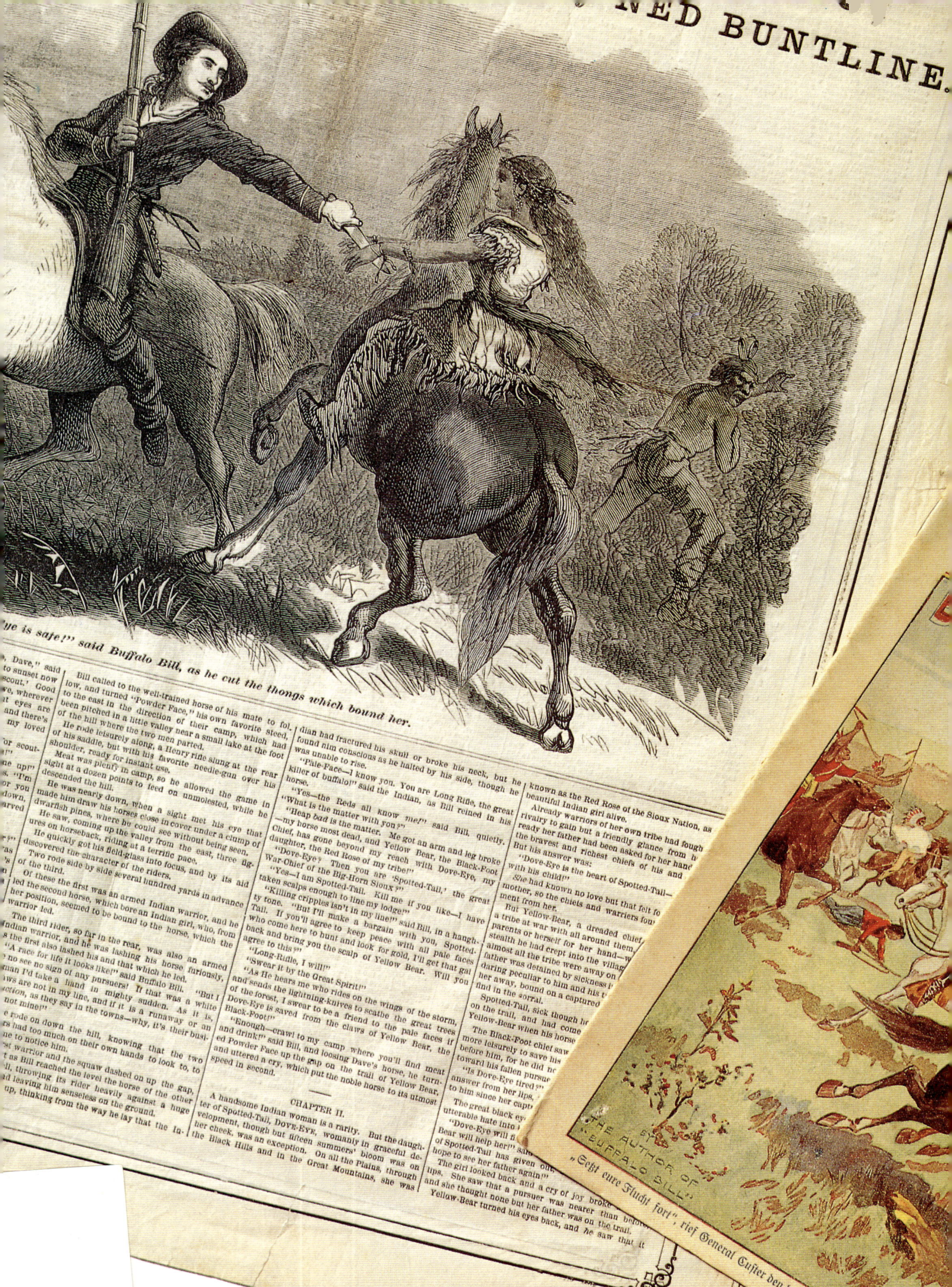
NED BUNTLINE.
ye is safe!" said Buffalo Bill, as he cut the thongs which bound her.
CHAPTER II.
BY THE AUTHOR OF "BUFFALO BILL"
„Setzt eure Flucht fort", rief General Custer den be

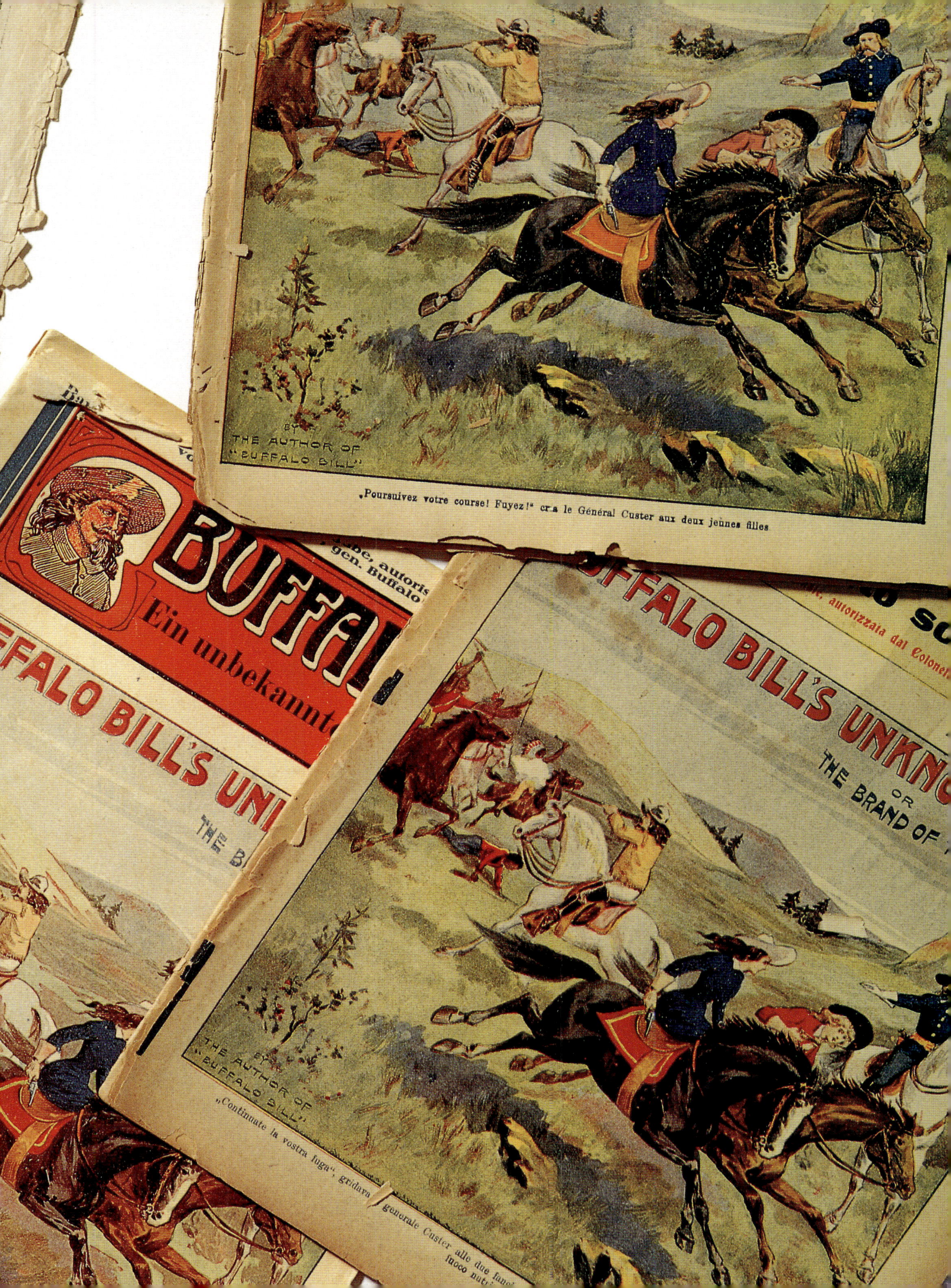
BY THE AUTHOR OF "BUFFALO BILL"
„Poursuivez votre course! Fuyez!" cria le Général Custer aux deux jeunes filles.
Ein unbekannt
FFALO BILL'S UNKN
OR THE BRAND OF
„Continuate la vostra fuga", gridava generale Custer alle due fanci

RIGHT:
TEA SET, STERLING SILVER, 1901.
A gift from Buffalo Bill, this tea set is inscribed, "Col. W. F. Cody to his niece Mary Jester, Duluth, 1901." A press agent for Buffalo Bill's Wild West, Mary Jester Allen went on to establish and direct the Buffalo Bill Museum.

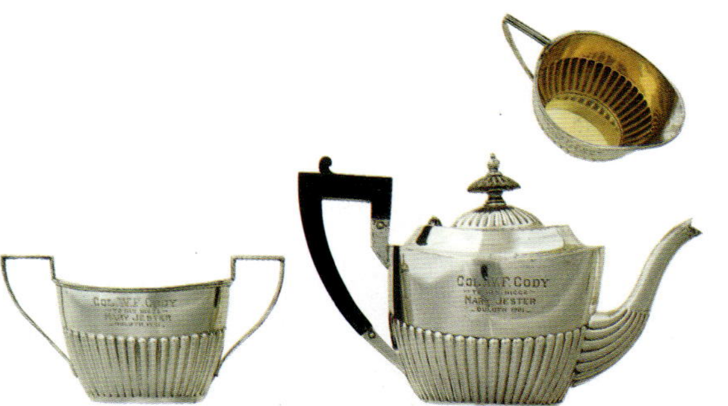

RIGHT:
BUFFALO BILL, 1871. MORA.
BLACK AND WHITE PHOTOGRAPH;
5-3/8 IN. X 4 IN.
Vincent Mercaldo Collection.

The museum which has grown into the world's finest institution devoted to Western American culture and history came to life as a modest entity in a small Western town. Legally established as the Buffalo Bill Memorial Association shortly after the death of William Frederick Cody in 1917, the Buffalo Bill Museum opened in 1927 in an elegant log building patterned after Cody's TE Ranch house. In the decades since, the collection has expanded to encompass memorabilia and mementos of Buffalo Bill, his Wild West show and the times in which he lived. In like manner, the original museum has now become the four museums and research library which comprise the Buffalo Bill Historical Center.

This book is the third in a series of five which began with the publication of *Cody Firearms Museum* in 1991. The second, *Treasures From Our West*, presents an overview of the four museums and the library. This volume, *Buffalo Bill Museum*, explores the life and times of William Frederick Cody, using objects from the collection of the Buffalo Bill Museum for illustrations. It reflects on the history of the West, the importance of cultural objects in history's interpretation and the role of Cody in that story.

We hope you enjoy this book. Furthermore, we hope reading it will inspire you to join the museum's growing family, the Patrons Association of the Buffalo Bill Historical Center. Come share in our efforts to preserve and interpret our distinctively Western heritage.

Peter H. Hassrick
Director

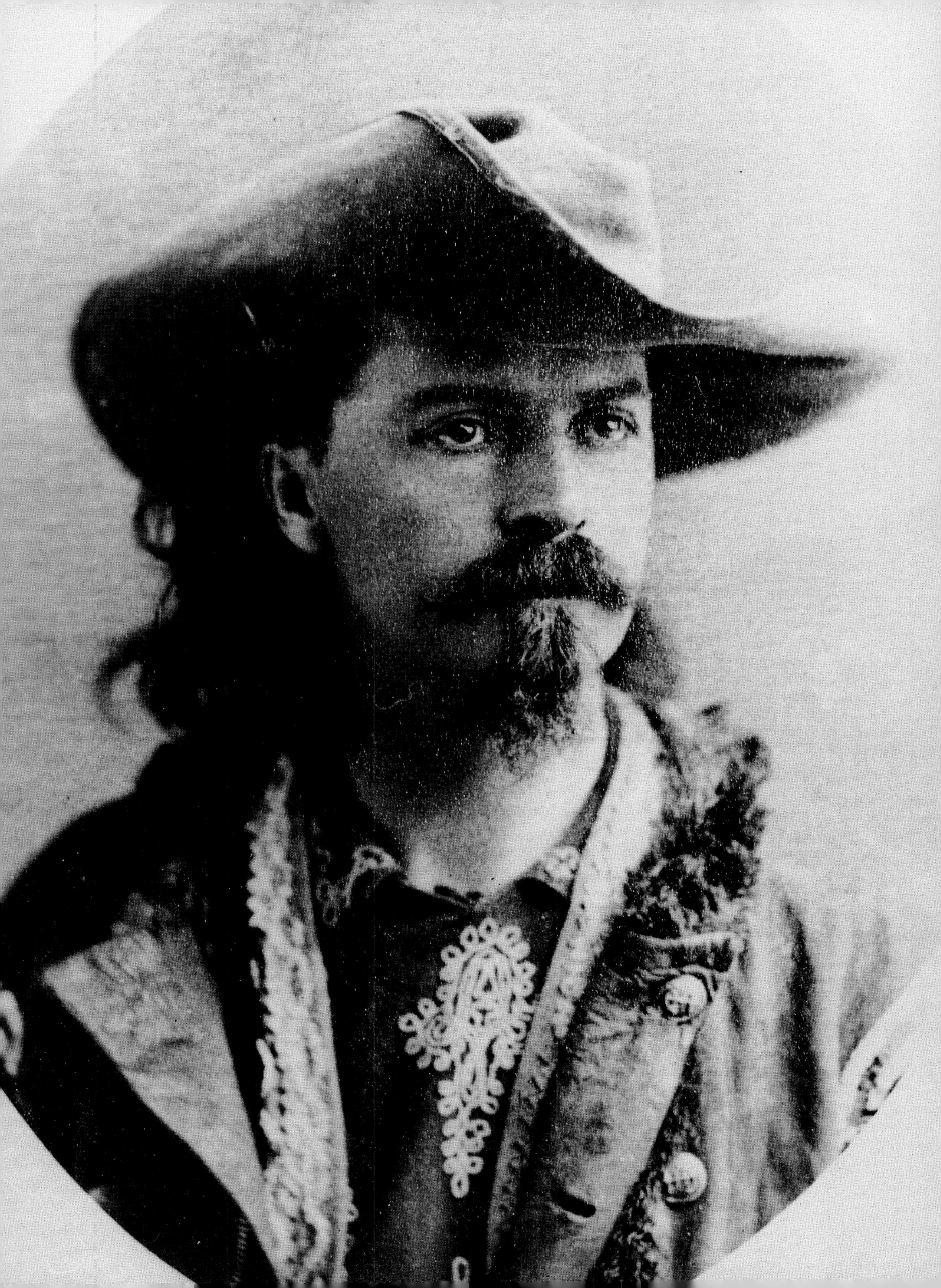

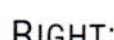

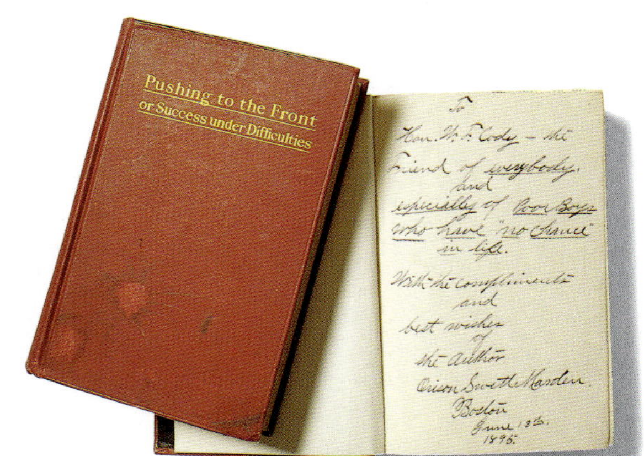

RIGHT:
PUSHING TO THE FRONT
BY ORISON SWETT MARDEN;
AUTOGRAPHED JUNE 1895.
This Horatio Alger-style tome was given to Buffalo Bill by the author, with an inscription that reads: "Hon. W.F. Cody—the Friend of *everyone* and especially of *Poor Boys* who have no chance in life."

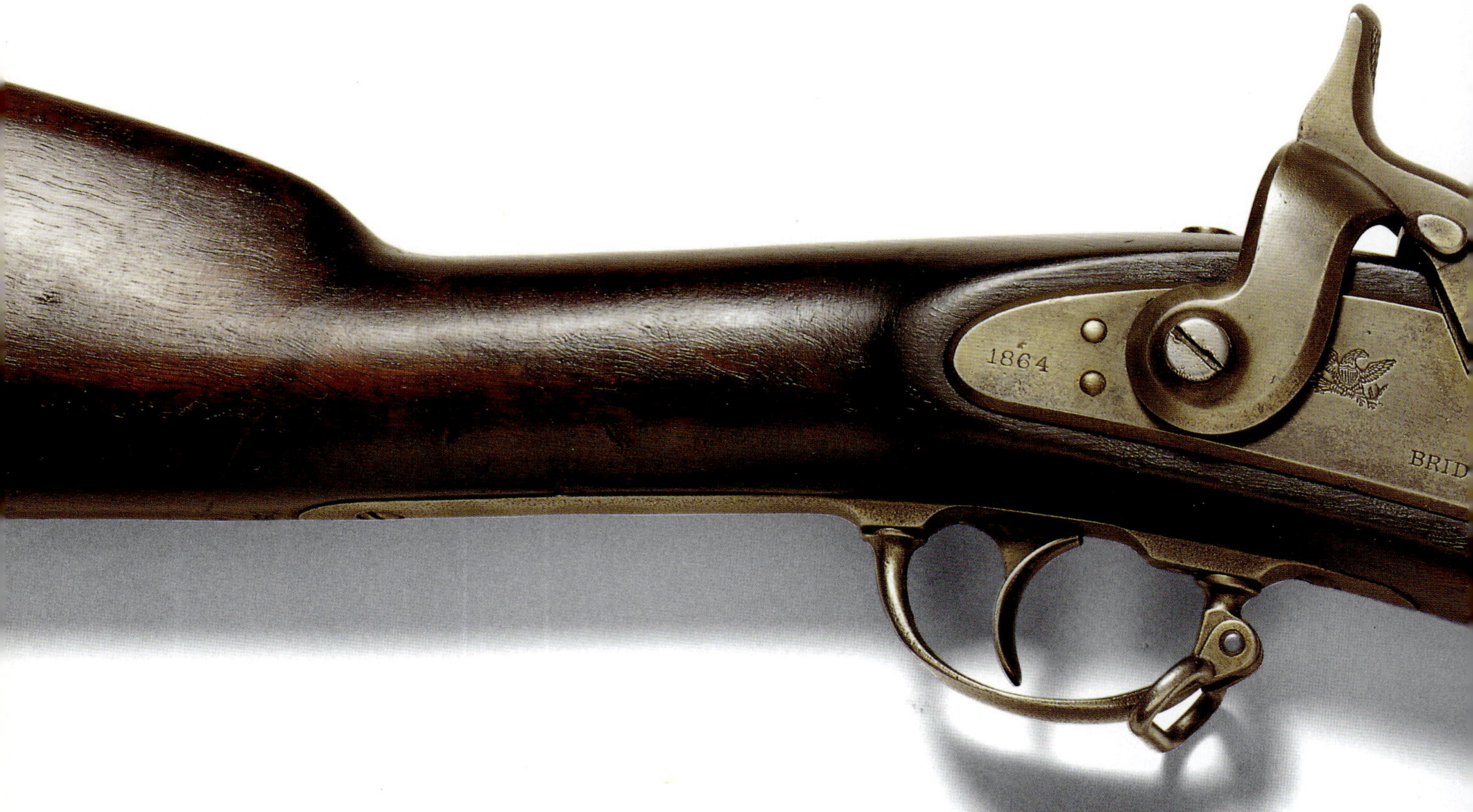

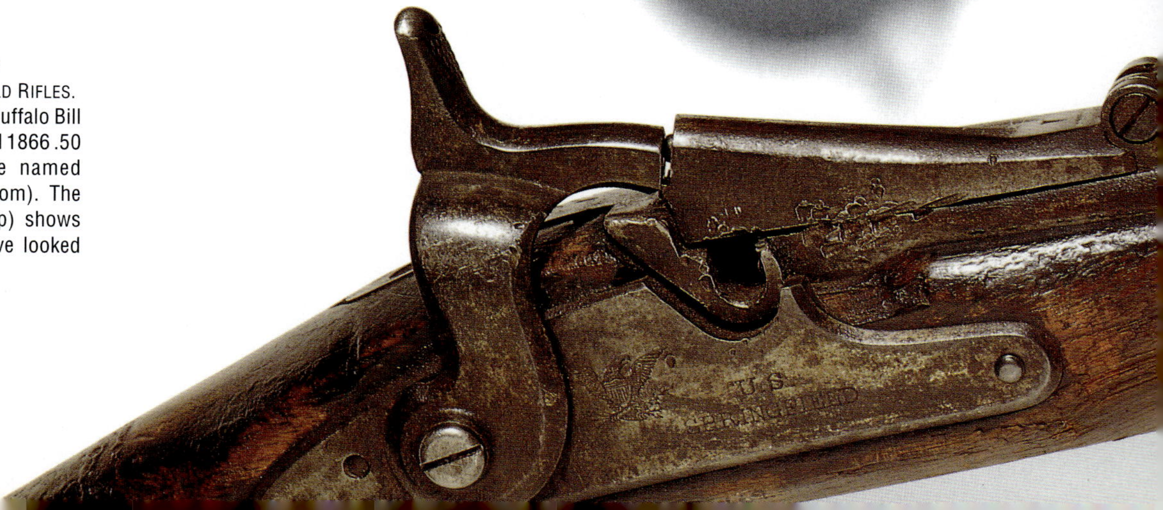

ABOVE:
SCOUT'S TOOLS:
MODEL 1866 SPRINGFIELD RIFLES.
As a scout and hunter, Buffalo Bill used a Springfield Model 1866 .50 caliber rifle which he named "Lucretia Borgia" (bottom). The other rifle pictured (top) shows what the rifle must have looked like when new.

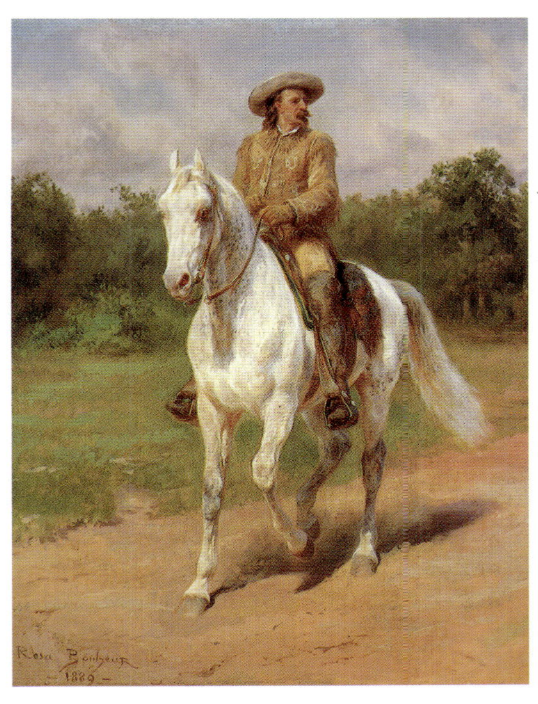

LEFT:
ROSA BONHEUR (1822-1899).
COL. WILLIAM F. CODY, 1889.
OIL ON CANVAS;
18 1/2 IN. X 15 1/4 IN.
GIFT OF ROBERT D. COE
IN MEMORY OF WILLIAM R. COE
AND MAI ROGERS COE.

When the Wild West show performed in Paris in 1889, well-known animal artist Rosa Bonheur produced 17 paintings of bison and other Western themes. Her portrait of him was one of Cody's favorites.

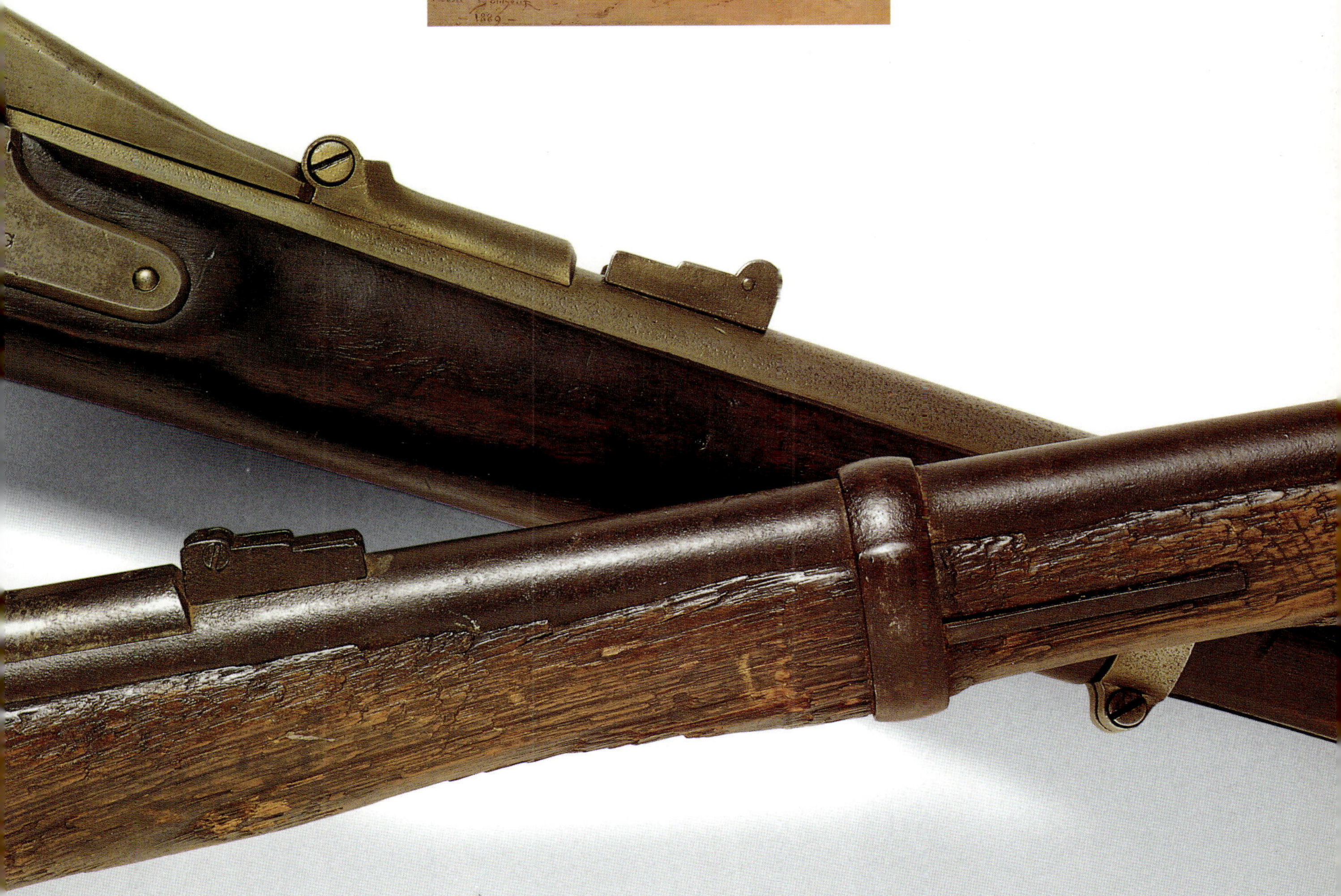

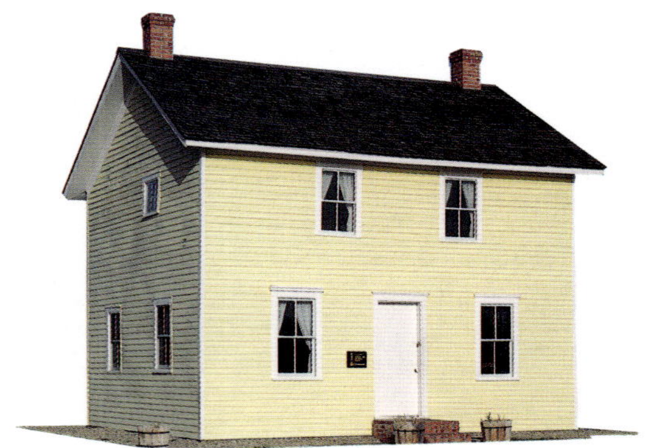

RIGHT:
BUFFALO BILL'S BOYHOOD HOME, BUILT IN LECLAIRE, IOWA, 1841.
The Cody family lived in this house for two years before moving to Kansas in 1854. The house was purchased by the Chicago, Burlington, and Quincy Railroad, moved to Cody in 1933, and given to the Buffalo Bill Memorial Association in 1948.

Iowa Territory was new when Isaac Cody moved his family there in 1840. By the time his second son, William Frederick, was born in 1846, Isaac was manager of a 600-acre farm near LeClaire which he had helped establish. Eight years later, he took his family west to Kansas where young Billy would grow up, attend school, trap beaver, and, after his father's death in 1857, work as a freight company express boy on a frontier continually striking farther onto the Great Plains.

RIGHT:
BUFFALO BILL, C. 1873.
ORIGINAL PHOTOGRAPH.

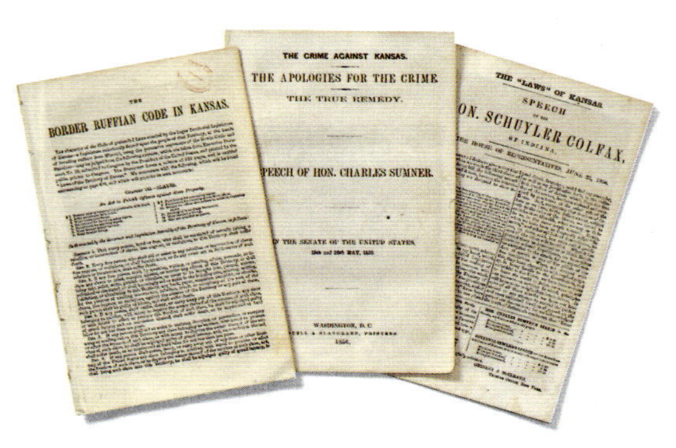

RIGHT:
POLITICAL PAMPHLETS:
THE "LAWS" OF KANSAS,
THE BORDER RUFFIAN CODE,
THE CRIME AGAINST KANSAS,
C. 1856.
The struggle for statehood known as "Bleeding Kansas" pitted slavery apologists against abolitionists. Even those who took no stand for or against southern slavery were often swept into the conflict. When Isaac Cody argued against allowing slavery in Kansas, he was harassed and stabbed.

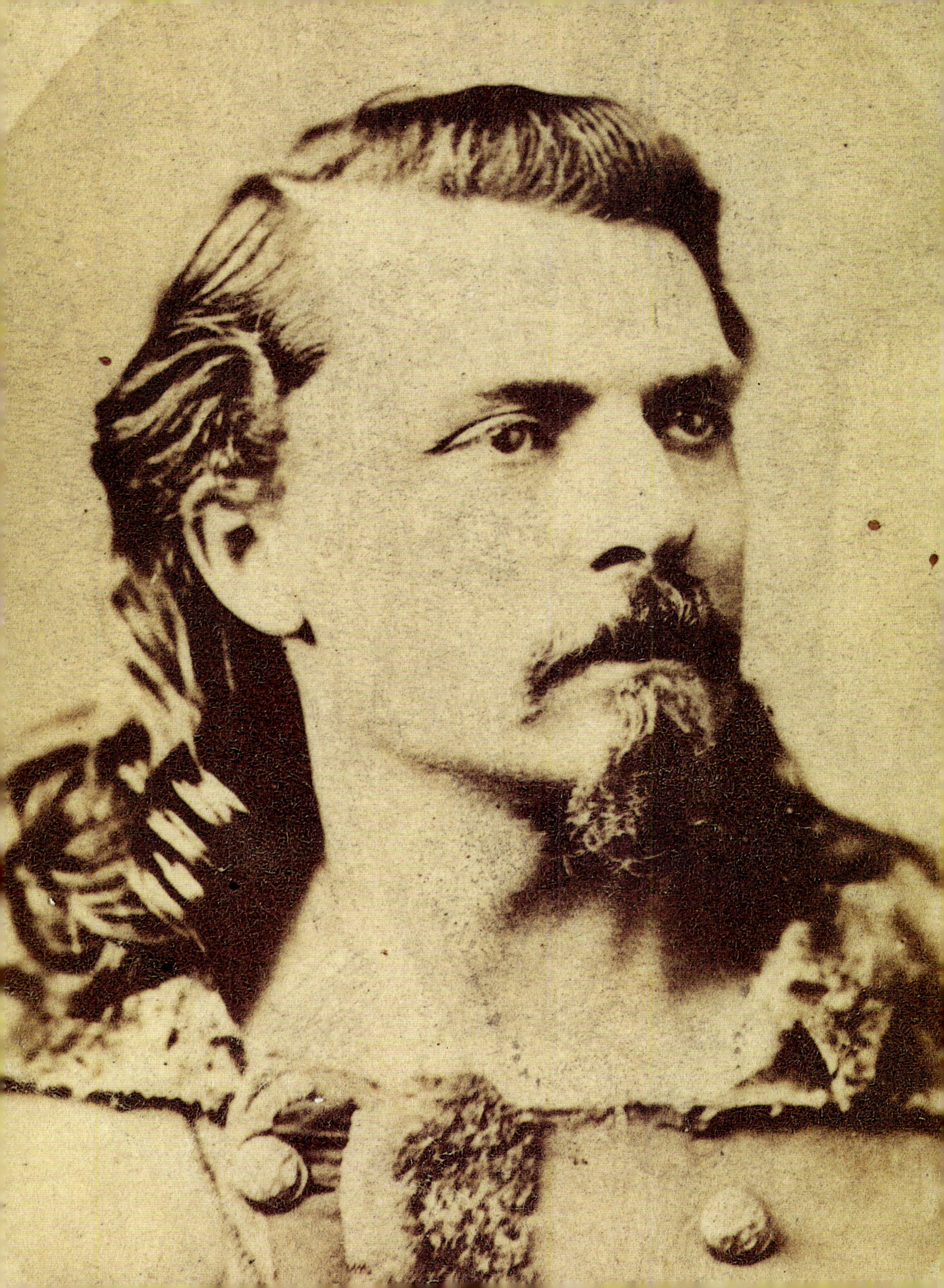

RIGHT:
DERRINGER PERCUSSION POCKET PISTOLS, 1865.
GIFT OF THE GERALD KLAZ FAMILY.
Inscribed "W. F. Cody, 1865," these Henry Derringer pistols were purchased by Buffalo Bill while he was a Union soldier with the Seventh Kansas Volunteer Cavalry. They were a gambler's weapon, and he may have bought them in imitation of his friend and comrade-in-arms, James B. "Wild Bill" Hickok.

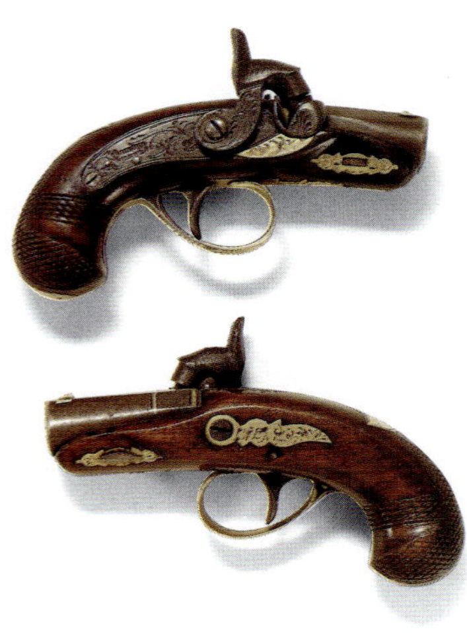

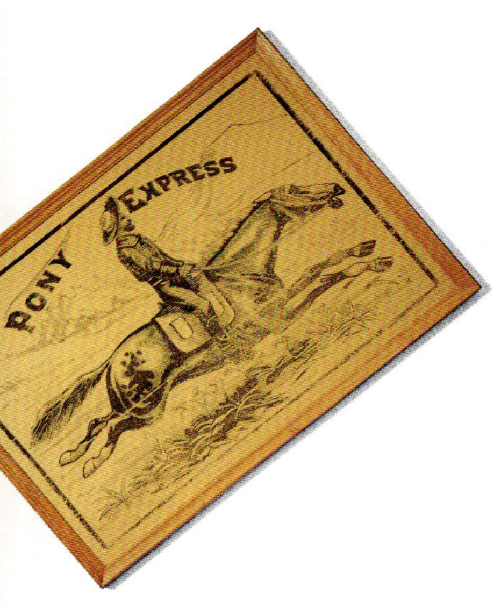

Frontiersman, hunter, scout, showman, and entrepreneur, Buffalo Bill Cody followed the same frontier that so many of his contemporaries saw as a path to wealth and independence. At the age of 12, he worked for a wagon train going to Fort Laramie; one year later he participated in the gold rush to Colorado; at age 15, he rode for the Pony Express. By the end of his life, he had come to symbolize the frontier itself.

But Cody was also drawn to the theaters and high society of the East. After fighting with the Union's Seventh Kansas Cavalry during the last years of the Civil War, he married Louisa Frederici, whom he had met in St. Louis. While Cody began to forge a career for himself in theater, he and Louisa lived for a time near West Chester, Pennsylvania, and in Rochester, New York, before finally settling at North Platte, Nebraska, in 1878. Of four children, a daughter, Orra Maude, and an only son, Kit Carson, died in childhood and are buried in Rochester. Partly because Cody spent years on the road, his turbulent relationship with Louisa almost ended in divorce in 1905.

ABOVE:
PONY EXPRESS ADVERTISING WOODCUT
(MAY HAVE ADVERTISED A BOOK ABOUT THE PONY EXPRESS).
The Pony Express operated for just 18 months from 1860 to 1861. The riders' youth—their average age was 19—endurance, and fabled speed became central to America's Western myth. Each ride covered about 75 miles, with a stop for fresh horses every 10 to 15 miles. The result: mail sent from Missouri to California by Pony Express reached its destination in ten days.

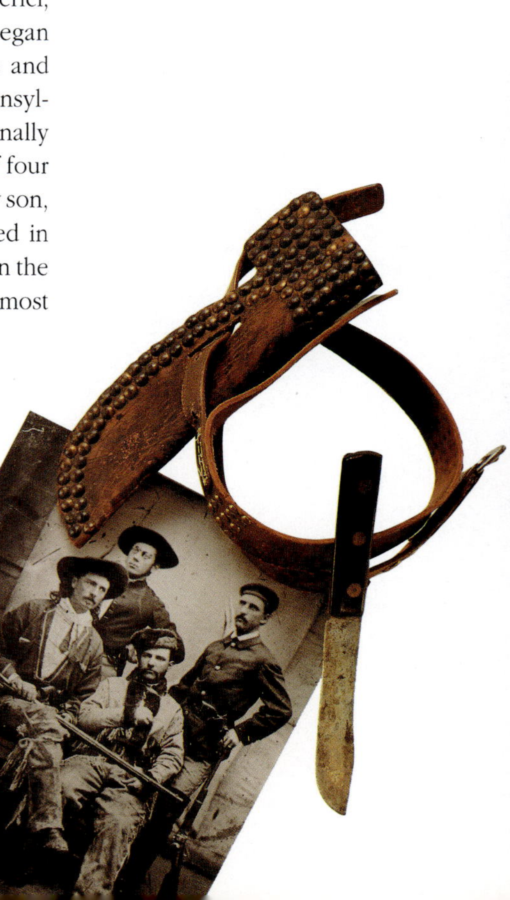

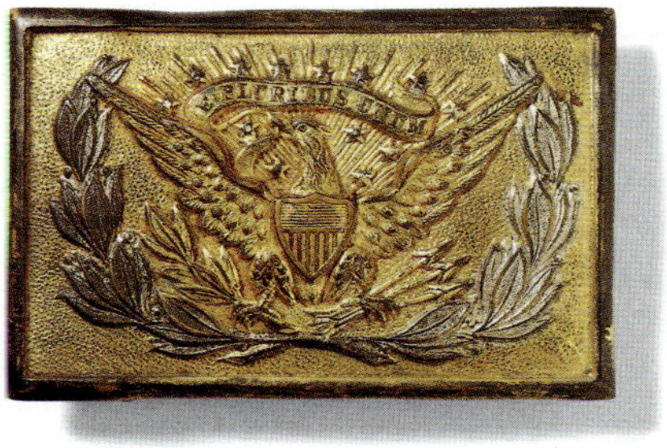

Above:
Union Army Uniform Buckle,
c. 1864.
Belonged to W.F. Cody.

Cody observed the Civil War up close in 1864-1865. He had occasionally scouted for the Army but promised his mother he would not enlist while she was alive. Three months after her death he was mustered into the Seventh Kansas Volunteer Cavalry and later saw action at the Battles of Tupelo and Pilot Knob.

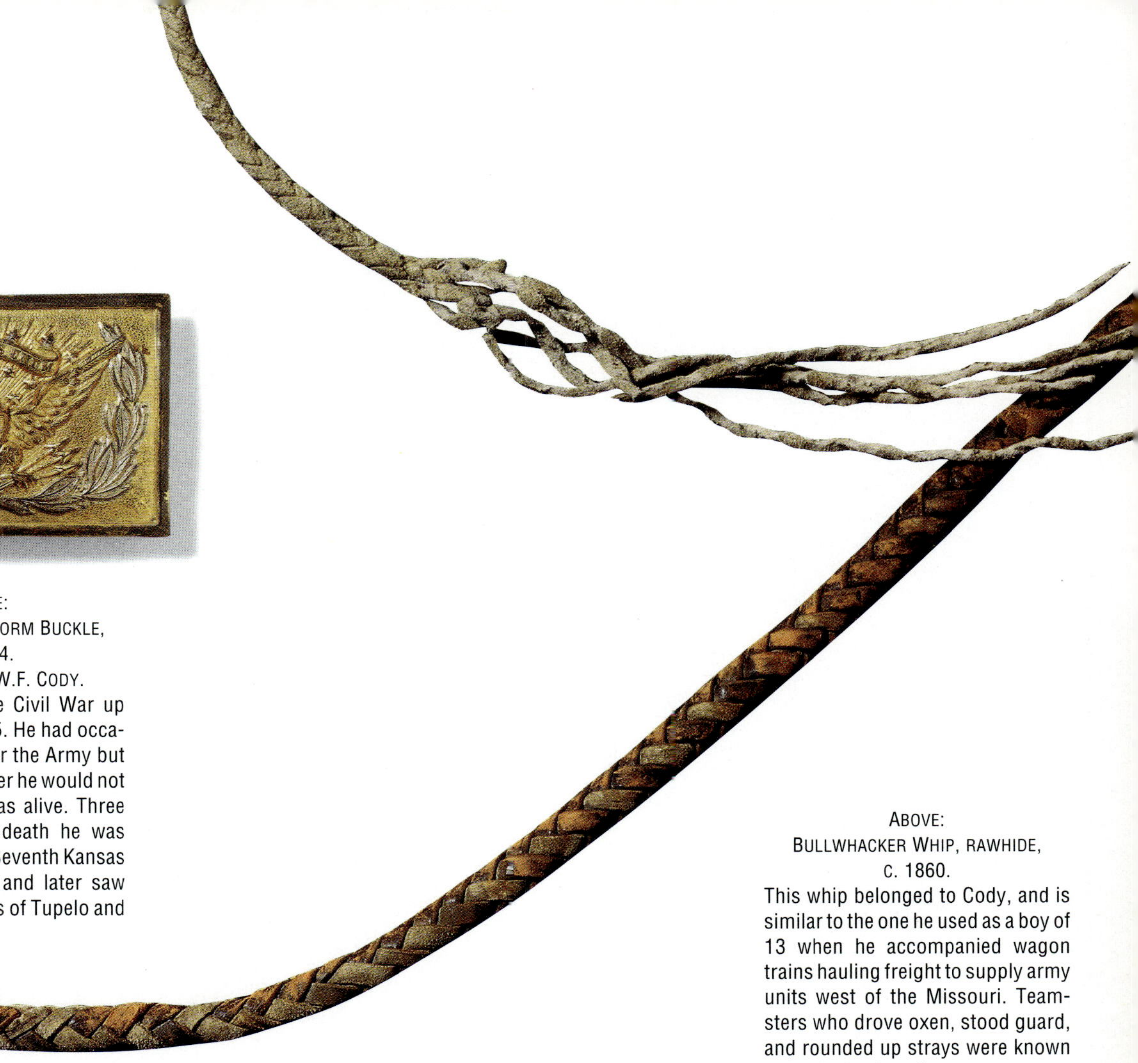

Above:
Bullwhacker Whip, rawhide,
c. 1860.

This whip belonged to Cody, and is similar to the one he used as a boy of 13 when he accompanied wagon trains hauling freight to supply army units west of the Missouri. Teamsters who drove oxen, stood guard, and rounded up strays were known as "bullwhackers."

Right:
Mochila, brown leather with brass catches and locks, 1897.

Used by the Pony Express, mochilas like this had four locked pockets or "cantinas" for carrying mail. No original Pony Express mochilas are known to exist; this replica was made by Louis Hook of Salt Lake City in 1897 and may have been used in the Wild West show.

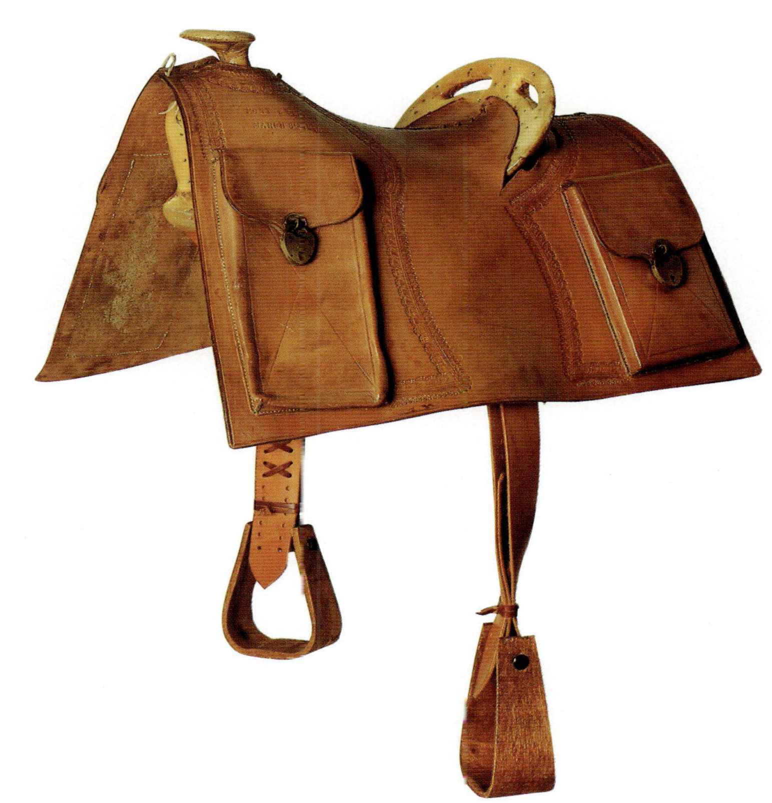

Left:
Buffalo Bill as a Scout, 1869.
Photograph from original tintype.
Gift of Mr. and Mrs. Fred Garlow.

In the earliest photograph known of Cody during his scouting days, he sits (left) with Lucretia Borgia, his Springfield rifle, across his lap. Two officers stand behind Cody, and an unidentified scout sits at his right.

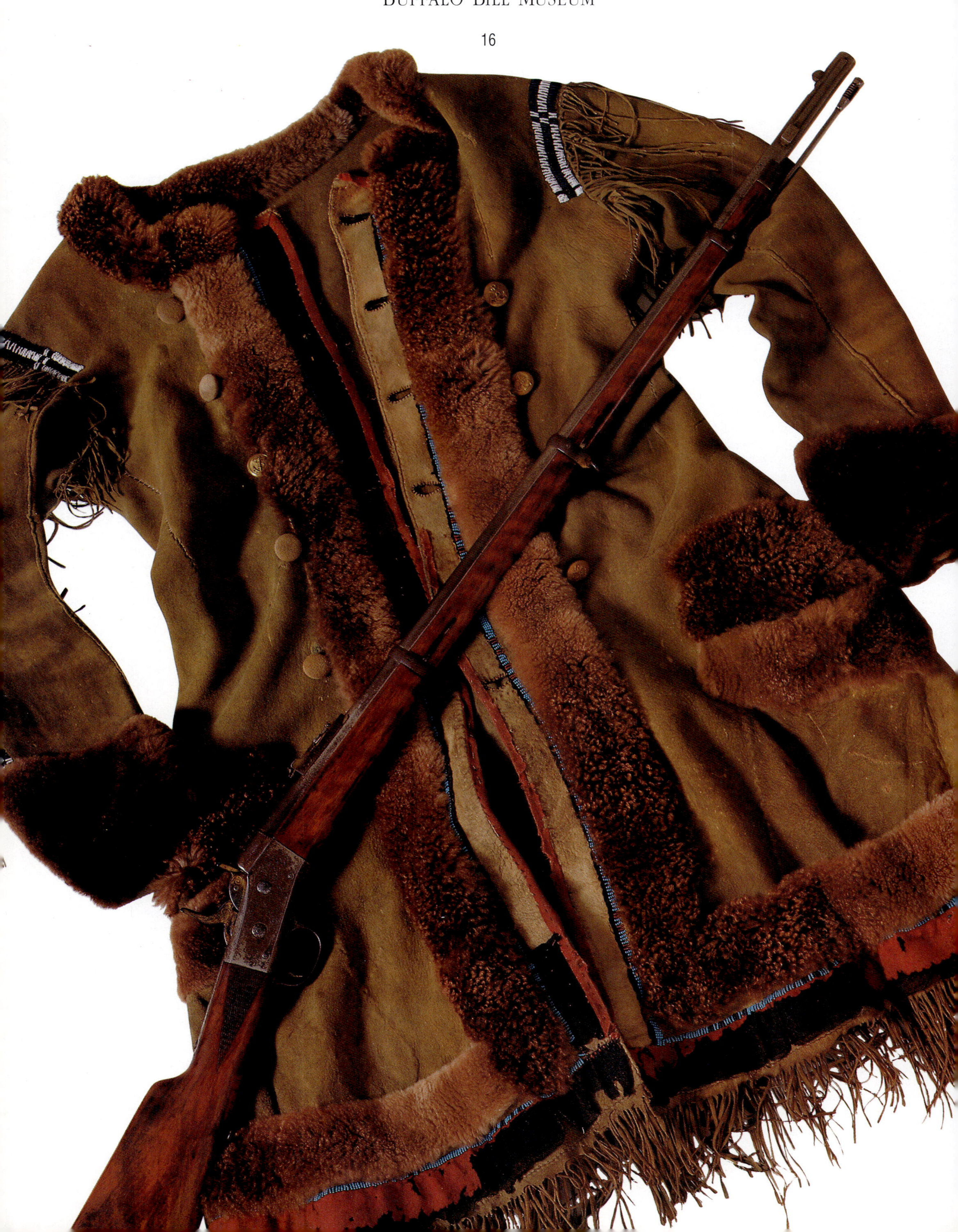

RIGHT:
COLT MODEL 1873 SINGLE-ACTION REVOLVERS, .45 CALIBER, 1880.
GIFT OF WILLIAM F. SCHNEIDER.
This set of ivory-gripped revolvers was a gift from Buffalo Bill to William F. Schneider, a fellow actor with the Buffalo Bill combination theater troupe. He and Cody exchanged numerous gifts, and Schneider emulated Cody's manner and style of dress.

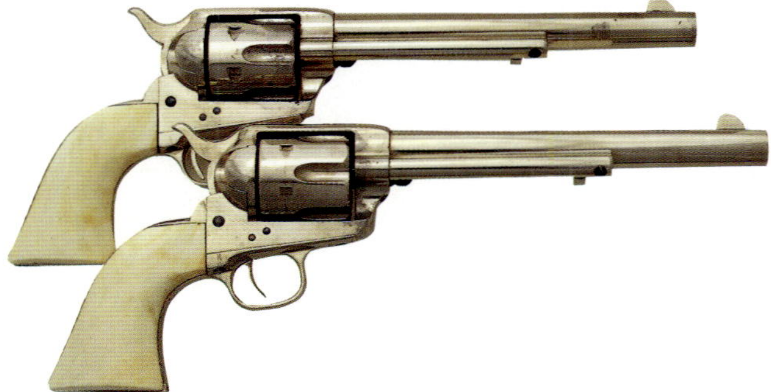

BELOW:
CONGRESSIONAL MEDAL OF HONOR, 1872.
Buffalo Bill was awarded the Medal of Honor for valor during a skirmish with the Sioux on April 26, 1872, east of North Platte, Nebraska. His name, like those of four other scouts, was stricken from the Army's Medal-of-Honor rolls in 1916 because he was a civilian at the time of the action. It was restored in 1989.

In the decade immediately following the Civil War, railroads and railroad building dominated the West's nascent economy. Boomtowns and commerce followed the rails, since laborers needed food and supplies. In 1867, Cody began hunting buffalo for Kansas Pacific work crews, thereby earning his nickname and his reputation as an expert shot.

When the U.S. Army employed him the next year as a civilian scout and guide for the Fifth Cavalry, Cody's experience as a plainsman, his survival skills, and his marksmanship made him an invaluable tracker and fighter. In 1872, he became one of only four civilian scouts to be awarded the Congressional Medal of Honor during the Indian Wars for valor in action.

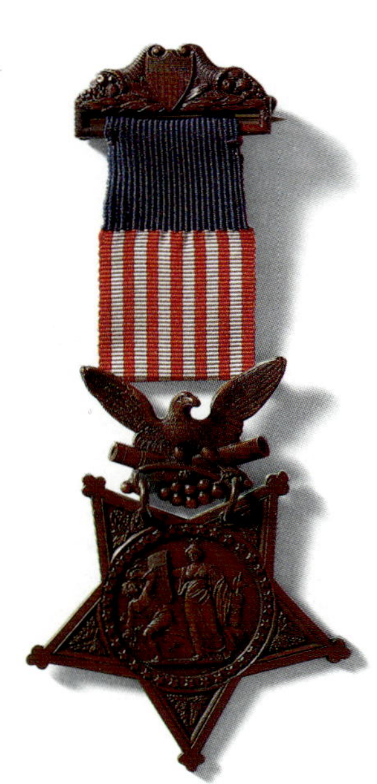

LEFT:
BUFFALO HIDE COAT WITH BEAVER TRIM, 1871,
AND REMINGTON MODEL 1866 RIFLE.
RIFLE GIFT OF MR. HARRY SCHLOSS,
GRANDSON OF MOSES KERNGOOD.
Though less supple than cloth, buffalo hide was warmer and more durable. Cody chose outfits like this beaded and beaver-trimmed coat that were not only practical but also eye-catching. Cody gave the rifle to his friend Moses Kerngood, a Rochester, New York, clothier.

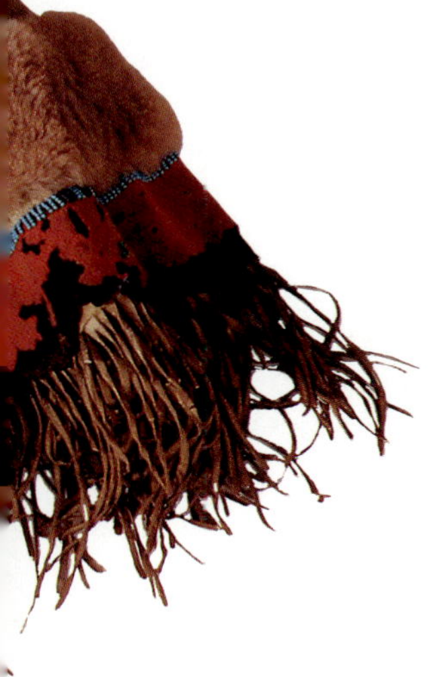

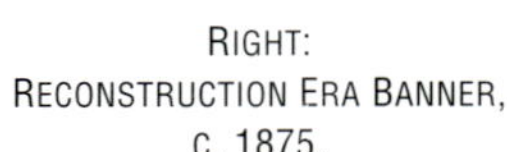

RIGHT:
RECONSTRUCTION ERA BANNER,
C. 1875.
The Civil War left indelible national scars. Reconstruction was an effort to restore the South's political and economic systems and to establish equal rights and opportunities for the freed slaves. It was also seen by many as an effort to punish the former Confederacy, and its enforcement exacerbated tensions between North and South. For many, the West alone represented American unity of culture and purpose.

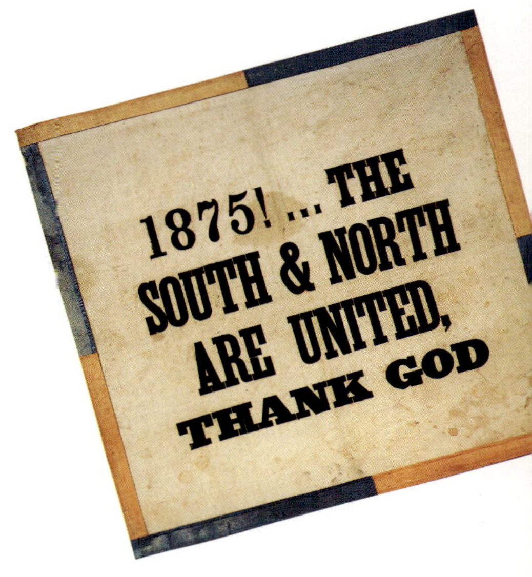

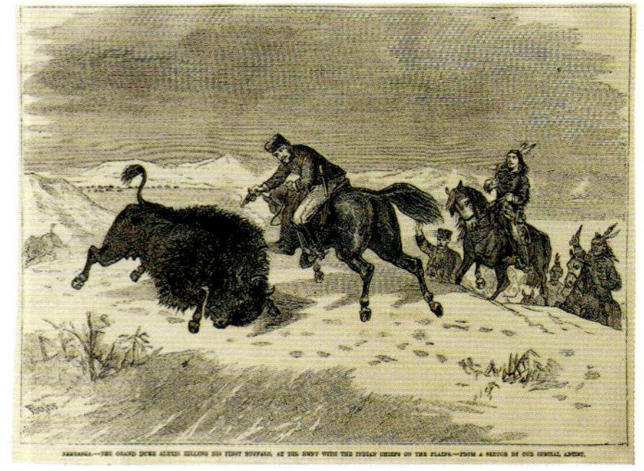

RIGHT:
FRANK LESLIE'S ILLUSTRATED,
FEBRUARY 3, 1872.
After 1865, interest in military matters plummeted. But the hunting expedition of Grand Duke Alexis of Russia, under the protection of the U.S. Army, was an all-out media event. Escorted by General Philip Sheridan and Brevet Major General George A. Custer, among others, and with Buffalo Bill as guide, the Russian visit glamorized the military as well as Buffalo Bill.

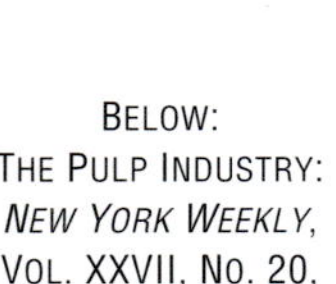

BELOW:
THE PULP INDUSTRY:
NEW YORK WEEKLY,
VOL. XXVII, NO. 20,
MARCH 25, 1872.
The *New York Weekly* was an eight-page tabloid publishing jokes, gossip columns, and serialized dime novels. All too often, Buffalo Bill in fictionalized form was treated as the larger-than-life hero. By 1900 one billion words had been printed about him in the popular press.

Despite the romance that surrounds it today, the post-Civil War Army had few friends, and frontier skirmishes often generated little interest east of the Mississippi. But when General Phil Sheridan enlisted Buffalo Bill's scouting expertise for non-military purposes, he sensed in Cody a combination of wilderness know-how and charisma that would reap a public relations windfall. Cody soon became a popular hunting guide for visiting dignitaries traveling under the Army's protection. Press coverage resulting from these often lavish expeditions turned Buffalo Bill into a celebrity, both in the United States and overseas.

Public interest in the West was sustained by journalists, novelists, and other media mavens. The dime novel press, especially, glamorized the plains and the supposed heroes and villains who lived there. Pulp novelist Ned Buntline was among those who made his living trying to read public sentiment. He saw that Buffalo Bill might become a central figure for Western enthusiasts and persuaded him to appear as himself in a stage play, *The Scouts of the Prairie.* Unfortunately, critics panned the "execrable" acting of Cody and fellow scout, co-star Texas Jack Omohundro.

Audiences, however, were more receptive. Buffalo Bill cut a dashing figure with his sombrero and fringed buckskin jacket; his faux pas and miscues became part of his rustic persona. As an actor, Cody toured the country with his own "combination" each fall and winter of the next ten years.

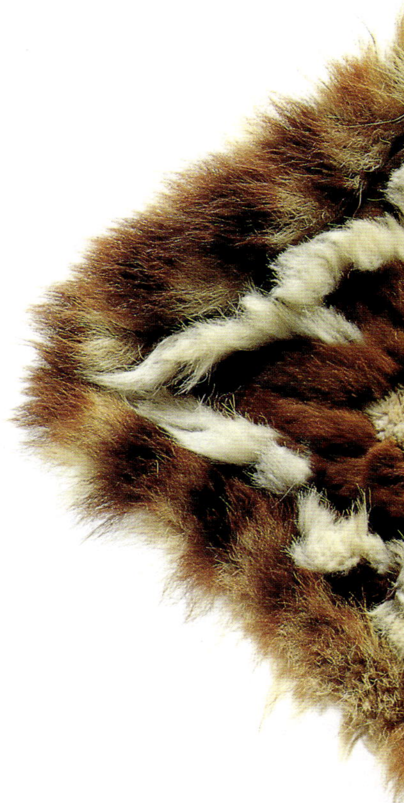

RIGHT:
DETAIL, FUR CARRIAGE ROBE,
C. 1872.
GIFT OF SAMUEL REBER.
After the sale of Alaska to the United States, Russians and Americans envisioned a Pacific trading alliance that would rival European wealth. That Buffalo Bill only enhanced international relations when he guided the Grand Duke Alexis is amply attested to by the lavish gifts he received, such as this Russian fur robe.

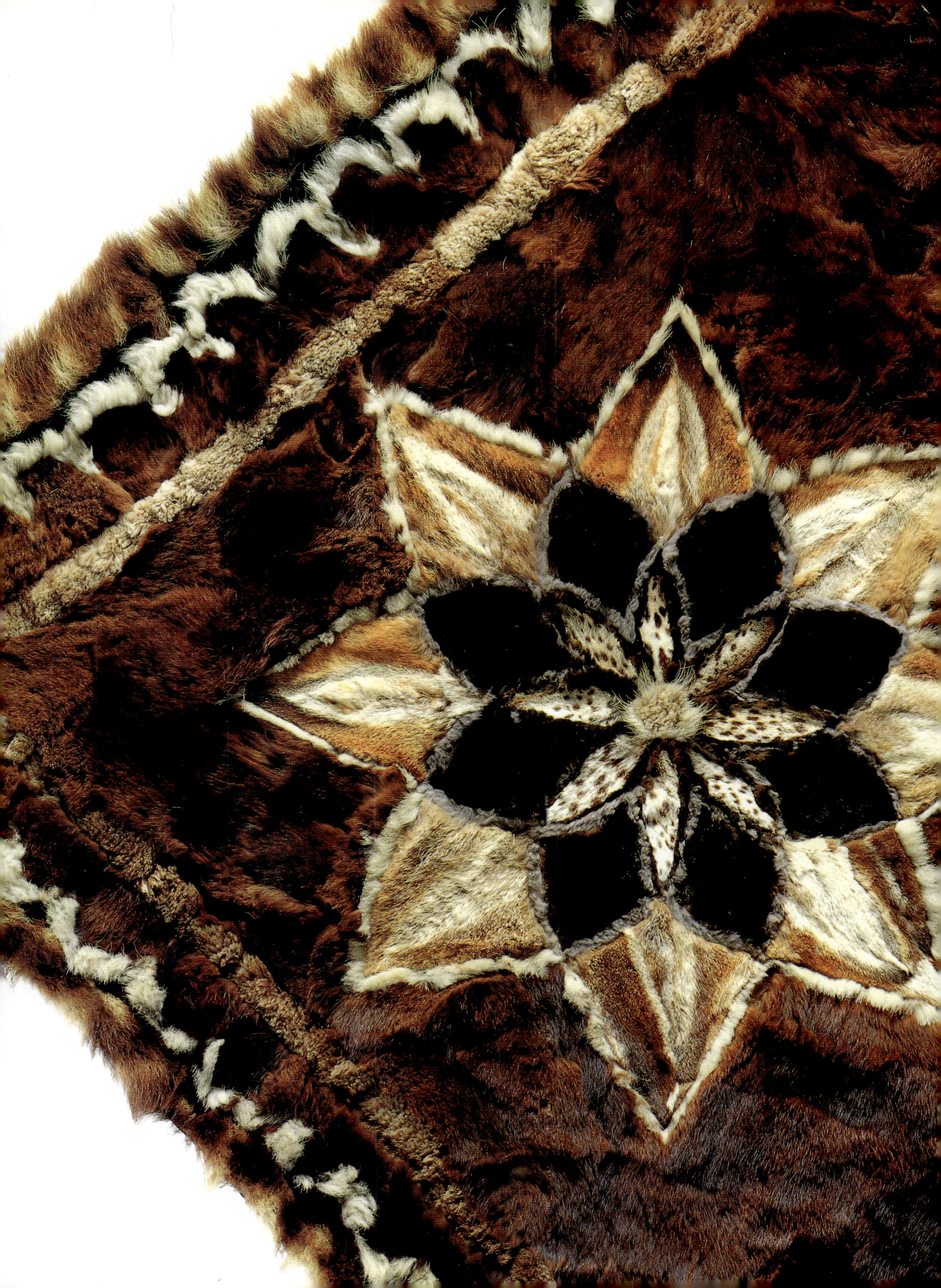

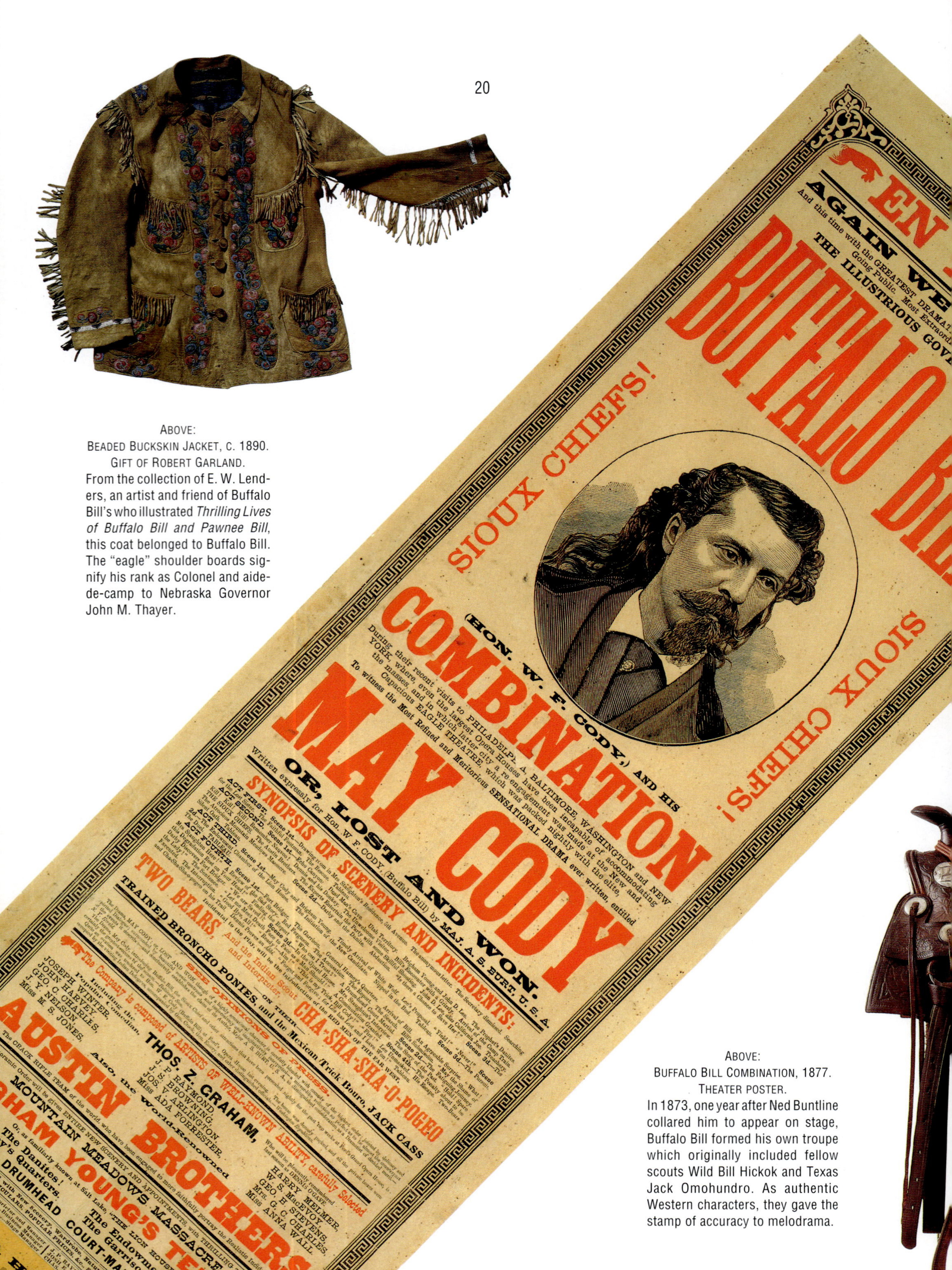

ABOVE:
BEADED BUCKSKIN JACKET, C. 1890.
GIFT OF ROBERT GARLAND.
From the collection of E. W. Lenders, an artist and friend of Buffalo Bill's who illustrated *Thrilling Lives of Buffalo Bill and Pawnee Bill*, this coat belonged to Buffalo Bill. The "eagle" shoulder boards signify his rank as Colonel and aide-de-camp to Nebraska Governor John M. Thayer.

ABOVE:
BUFFALO BILL COMBINATION, 1877.
THEATER POSTER.
In 1873, one year after Ned Buntline collared him to appear on stage, Buffalo Bill formed his own troupe which originally included fellow scouts Wild Bill Hickok and Texas Jack Omohundro. As authentic Western characters, they gave the stamp of accuracy to melodrama.

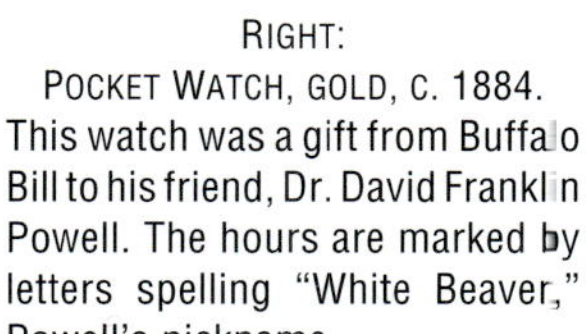

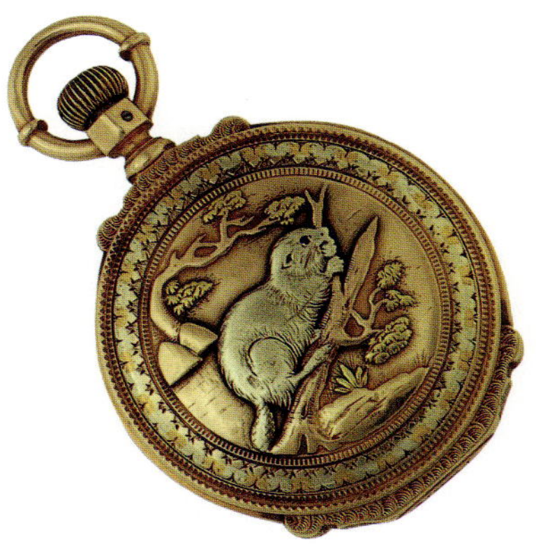

RIGHT:
POCKET WATCH, GOLD, C. 1884.
This watch was a gift from Buffalo Bill to his friend, Dr. David Franklin Powell. The hours are marked by letters spelling "White Beaver," Powell's nickname.

With the Army planning finally to crush the Plains Indians' resistance to white settlement, Cody returned in the summers to the prairie and to guiding the Fifth Cavalry. Just three weeks after the defeat of Custer and his troops at the Little Bighorn, and with Americans calling for retribution, Cody's regiment intercepted a band of Cheyenne on July 17, 1876. When Buffalo Bill, wearing his stage clothing, killed a warrior named Yellow Hair (often mis-translated as "Yellow Hand") and scalped him, he reportedly cried out, "First scalp for Custer!" His career as a celebrity and a scout thus dovetailed—Buffalo Bill the frontiersman had proven that Buffalo Bill the character was no mere actor.

When Cody left scouting, he envisioned a life for himself as a gentleman rancher; a short career in show business would provide all the financing he would need. In fact, he became the ultimate showman, one who had lived the roles he would play. For a July 4th celebration in North Platte, Nebraska, in 1882, Cody organized the "Old Glory Blow-out," a combination rodeo/bronc-busting/shooting contest and "Wild West" exhibition. The show's success was encouraging. In 1883, Cody's "The Wild West, Rocky Mountain, and Prairie Exhibition" began touring the country, presenting for audiences what the *Chicago Evening Post* called "the truth as it was." For the rest of his life, Cody would be recognized as an entertainer and interpreter of Western history.

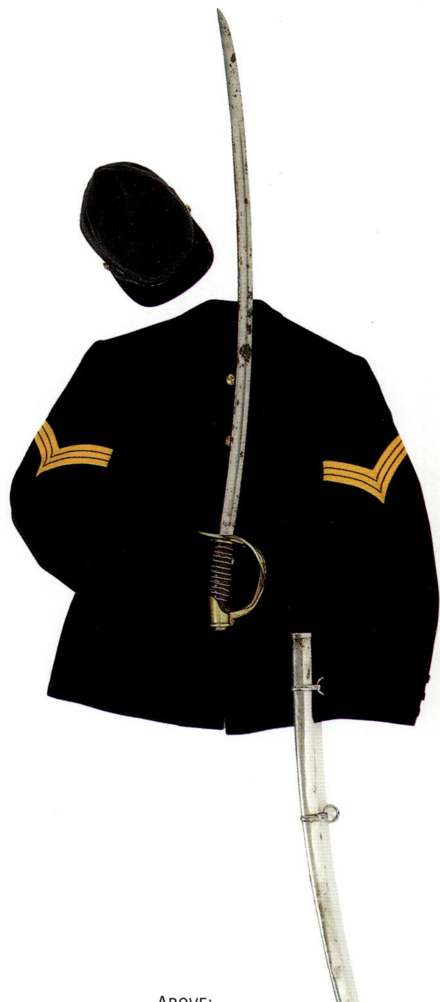

ABOVE:
CAVALRY SABER AND SCABBARD, MODEL 1860, AND
CAVALRY BLOUSE, 1875 PATTERN.
Because the post-war Army was generally underfunded and understaffed, Buffalo Bill's exploits as a scout in the Fifth Cavalry provided welcome publicity for the military.

BELOW:
SADDLE (WITH ANGORA SERAPE), BRIDLE, AND BEADED GAUNTLETS.
GAUNTLETS ARE A GIFT OF THE ISSUE OF JAMES M. ALLEN, SR. AND ALVA ISHAM ALLEN.
This Western gear belonged to Buffalo Bill. The saddle was made for him in 1893 by Collins and Morrison of Omaha.

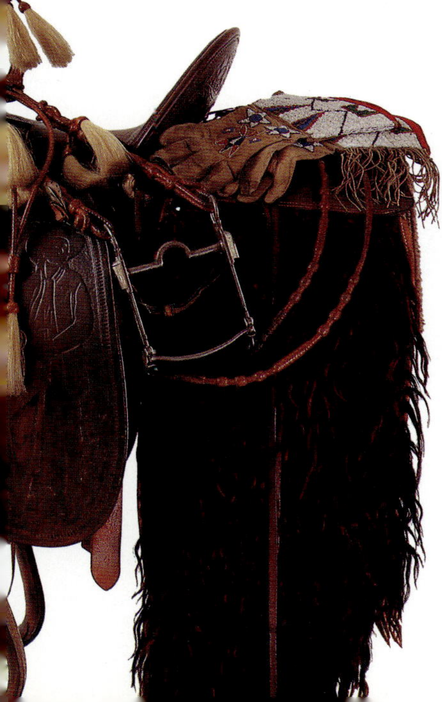

RIGHT:
CORPORATE SEAL, BUFFALO BILL'S WILD WEST AND PAWNEE BILL'S GREAT FAR EAST, 1912.
Cody invested in numerous projects from mining to tourism. The Wild West show, first incorporated in 1887, was a financial success for many years. In 1908, Pawnee Bill joined Buffalo Bill to form what was commonly referred to as "The Two Bills Show."

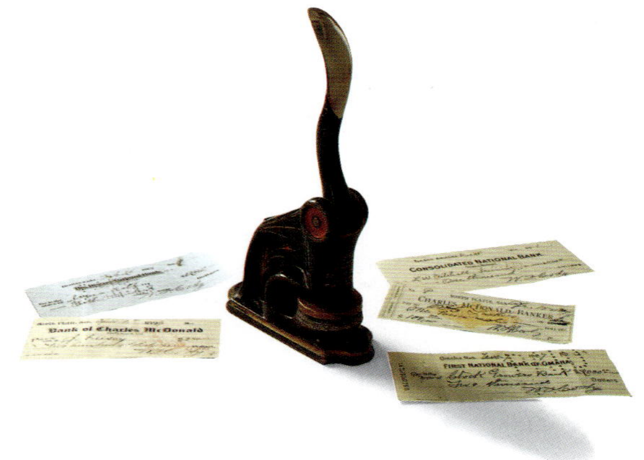

RIGHT:
VOTES FOR WOMEN, CAMPAIGN BUTTON.
Women employed by the Wild West show earned equal pay for equal work, and Cody was an early advocate of woman suffrage. In an 1894 interview he was asked if he believed the majority of women capable of voting. "Yes," he replied, "quite as much as the majority of men."

BELOW:
STOCK CERTIFICATES OF CODY-DYER ARIZONA MINING AND MILLING COMPANY, 1904 AND 1913.
In 1902, Cody joined in partnership with former Indian agent D. B. Dyer to develop mines in Pima County, Arizona. On March 13, 1903, a vein of tungsten-yielding ore was struck, but logistical problems kept the mine in constant debt.

Like other successful businesses, Buffalo Bill's Wild West show, as it came to be called, depended on advertising. For publicity, Cody received endorsements from generals under whom he had served, including Sheridan, Crook and Miles. He also worked with some of the country's largest printing houses to produce high-quality publicity posters. With his earnings, he invested in an Oracle, Arizona, tungsten mine, in a hotel in Sheridan, Wyoming, and in stock breeding, ranching, coal and oil development, film making, publishing, town building, and tourism. As a celebrity, Cody's arguments for women's rights and just treatment of American Indians were often quoted.

FAR RIGHT:
BUFFALO BILL'S HOTELS, ADVERTISING PAMPHLET, 1912.
Buffalo Bill tirelessly promoted the Cody area. In addition to his Pahaska Tepee hunting lodge near Yellowstone Park's east entrance, he owned a hotel in Wapiti, and put up $80,000 to build The Irma in Cody. Named after his youngest daughter, it offered steam heat, gas lighting, private telephones, and a barber shop.

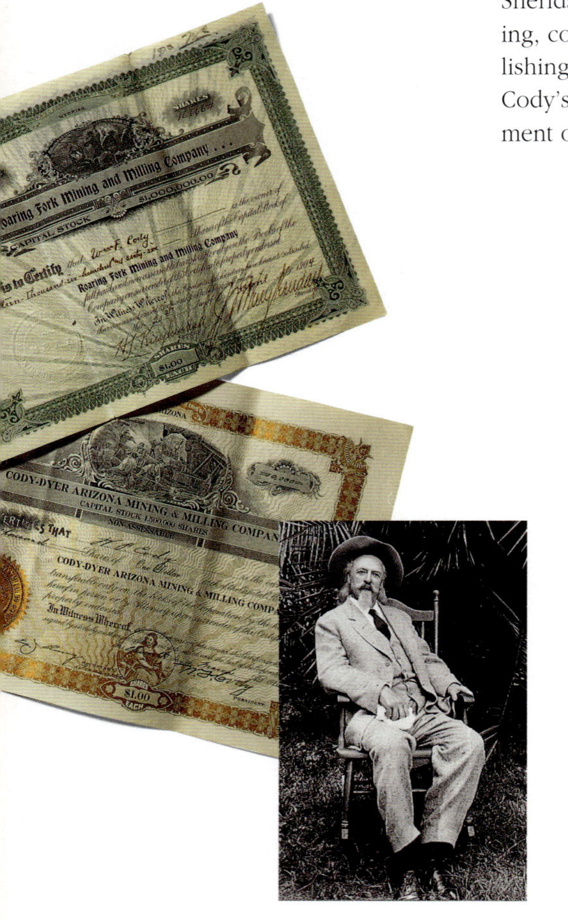

RIGHT:
LEDGER BOOK, SHERIDAN INN, 1894-1895.
GIFT OF MR. AND MRS. EUGENE BARKER.
Buffalo Bill first saw northern Wyoming in 1874, but as early as the 1860s Yale University paleontologist O. C. Marsh had described its geology to him. Eventually impressed by the area's tourist potential, he first invested in 1894 in a Sheridan, Wyoming, hotel.

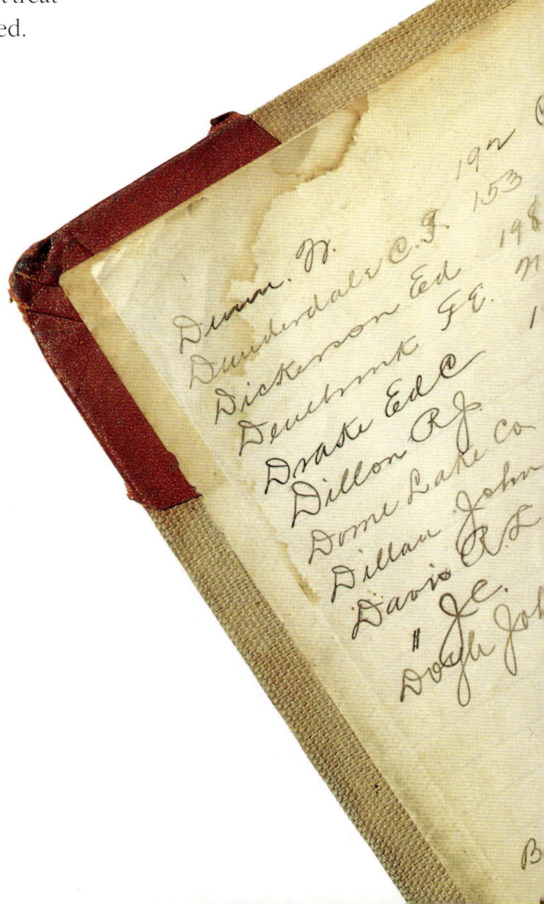

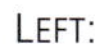

LEFT:
WILLIAM F. CODY, C. 1907.
ORIGINAL PHOTOGRAPH, FLORIDA.
Despite his characterization as a figure from the past, Buffalo Bill always looked to the future. As a businessman, he invested in projects he hoped might bring economic growth to the West.

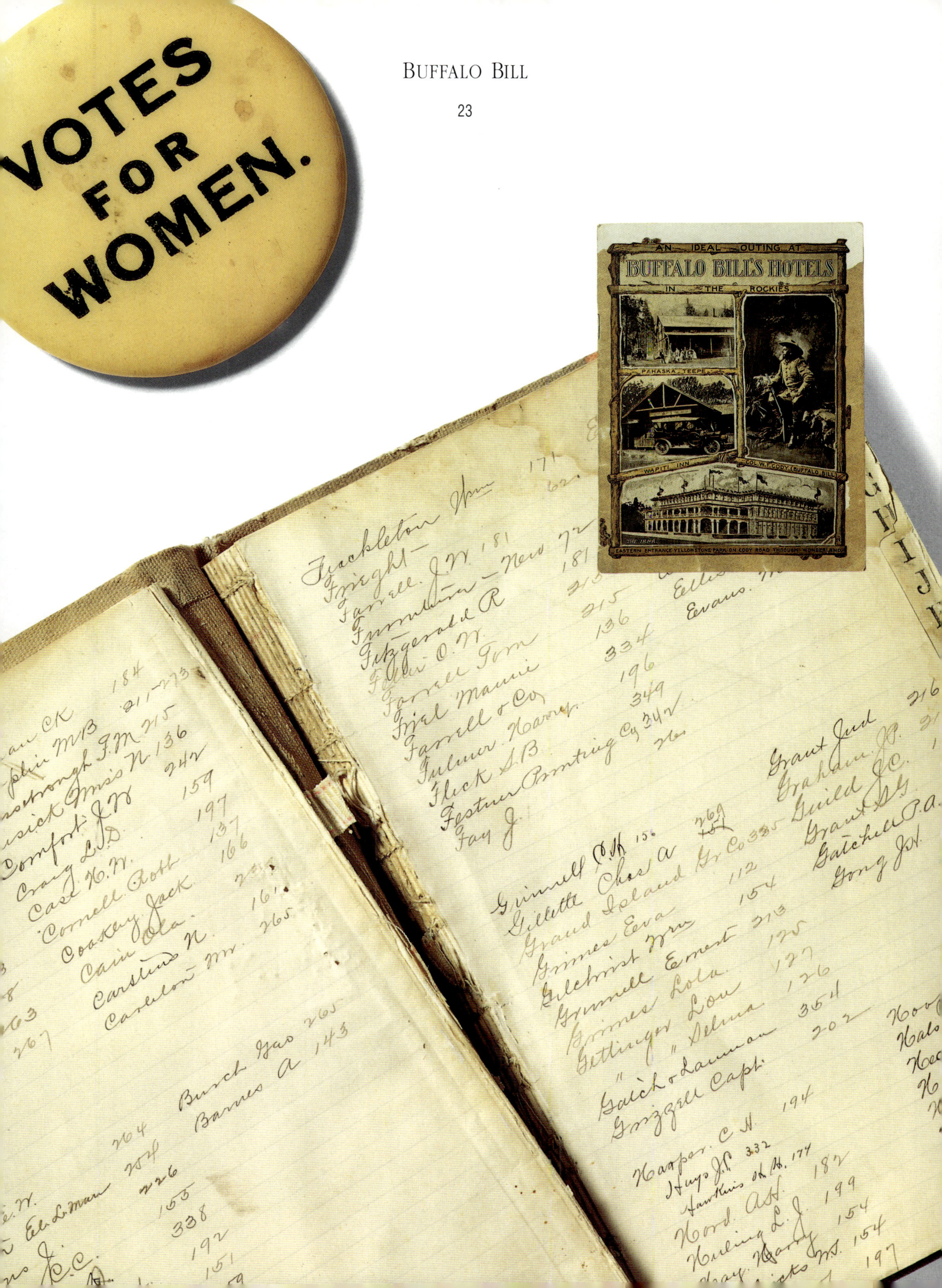
VOTES
FOR
WOMEN.
AN IDEAL OUTING AT
BUFFALO BILL'S HOTELS
IN THE ROCKIES
PAHASKA TEEPE
WAPITI INN
COL. W.F. CODY (BUFFALO BILL)
THE IRMA
EASTERN ENTRANCE YELLOWSTONE PARK ON CODY ROAD THROUGH WONDERLAND

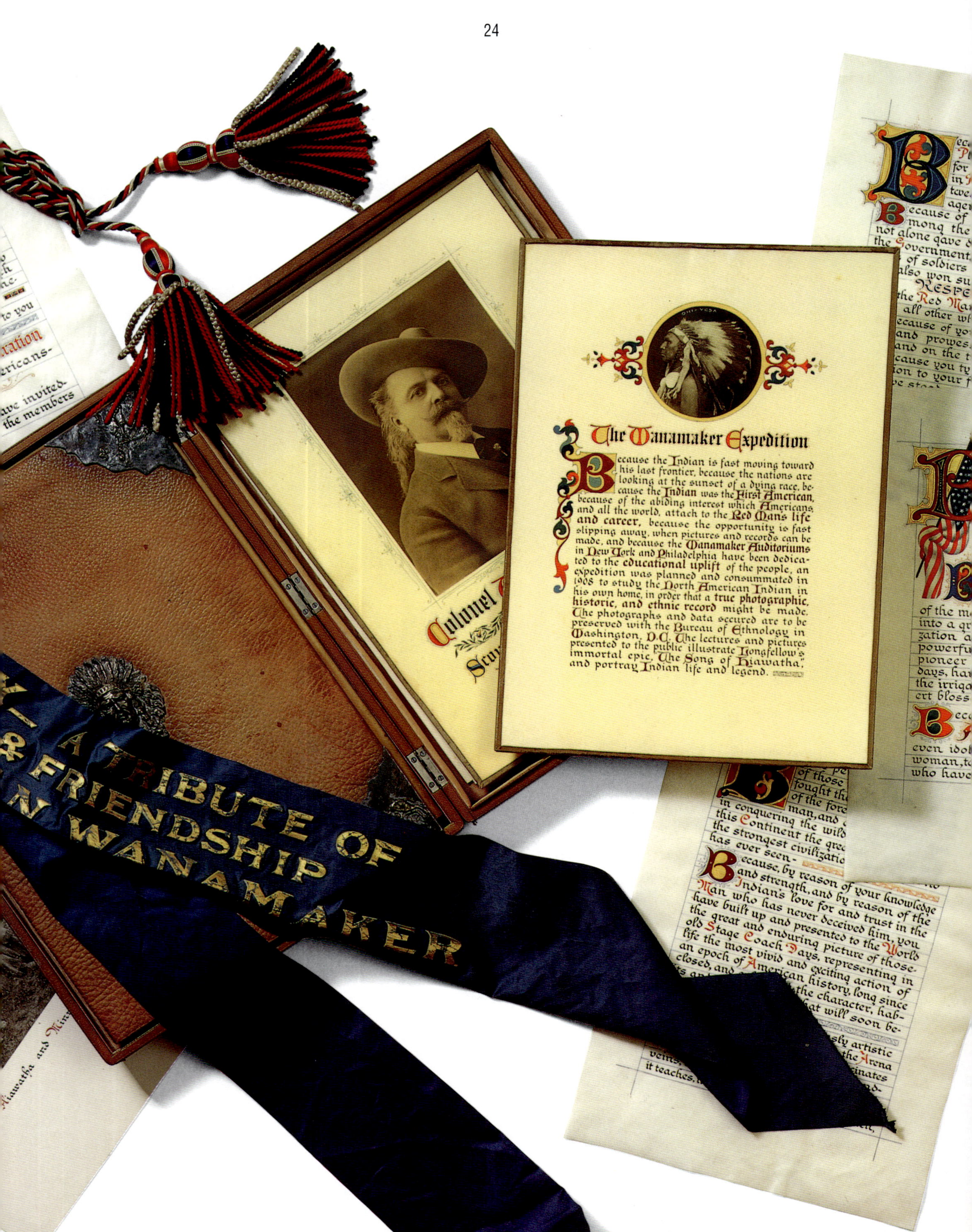
The Wanamaker Expedition
Because the Indian is fast moving toward his last frontier, because the nations are looking at the sunset of a dying race, because the Indian was the First American, because of the abiding interest which Americans, and all the world, attach to the Red Man's life and career, because the opportunity is fast slipping away, when pictures and records can be made, and because the Wanamaker Auditoriums in New York and Philadelphia have been dedicated to the educational uplift of the people, an expedition was planned and consummated in 1908 to study the North American Indian in his own home, in order that a true photographic, historic, and ethnic record might be made. The photographs and data secured are to be preserved with the Bureau of Ethnology in Washington, D.C. The lectures and pictures presented to the public illustrate Longfellow's immortal epic, "The Song of Hiawatha," and portray Indian life and legend.
A TRIBUTE OF
FRIENDSHIP
WANAMAKER

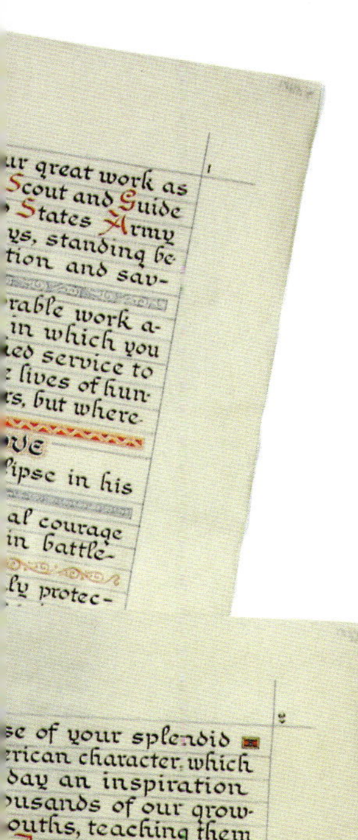

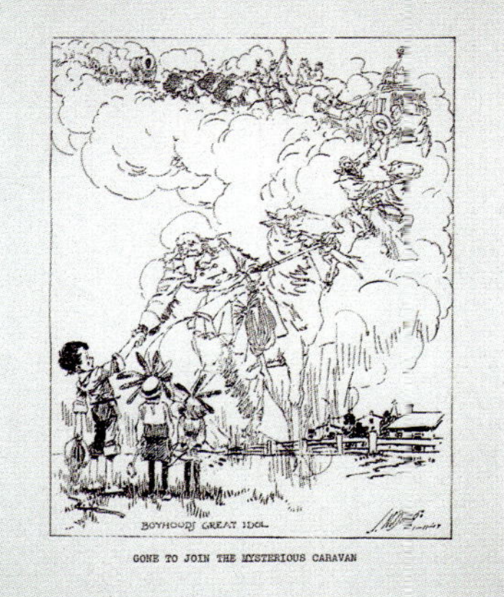

LEFT:
"BOYHOOD'S GREAT IDOL:
GONE TO JOIN THE MYSTERIOUS
CARAVAN." 1917. PRINTER'S PROOF,
J. N. "DING" DARLING CARTOON.
As dime novel hero and cultural icon, Buffalo Bill embodied raw courage and self-reliance. With his death, many children lost a direct connection to the fabled frontier era. A more famous cartoon modeled after this one appeared following the death of Theodore Roosevelt.

Like other westering entrepreneurs, Cody was instrumental in the development of the region's economy. Yet as Buffalo Bill—the man who personified the untamed frontier—he was primarily identified as a hero of the Old West.

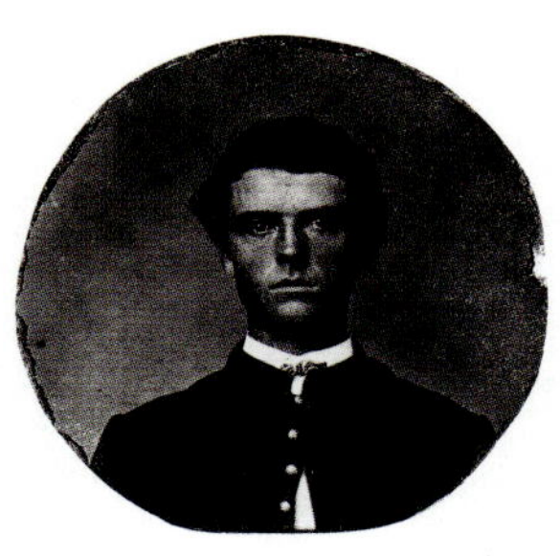

LEFT:
WANAMAKER BANNER AND
ILLUMINATED TESTIMONIAL, 1909.
Including Rinehart Indian photographs, this collection was presented to Cody for his role as a "friend of the Indian."

ABOVE:
PORTRAIT OF W. F. CODY, 1864.
REVERSED IMAGE FROM ORIGINAL
TINTYPE PHOTOGRAPH.
This picture shows 18-year-old Will Cody in his uniform blouse not long after he enlisted in the Union Army.

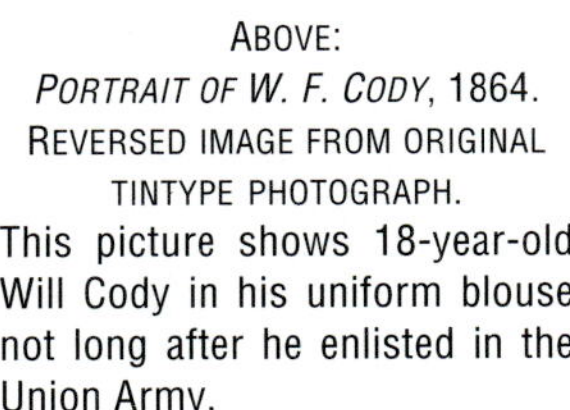

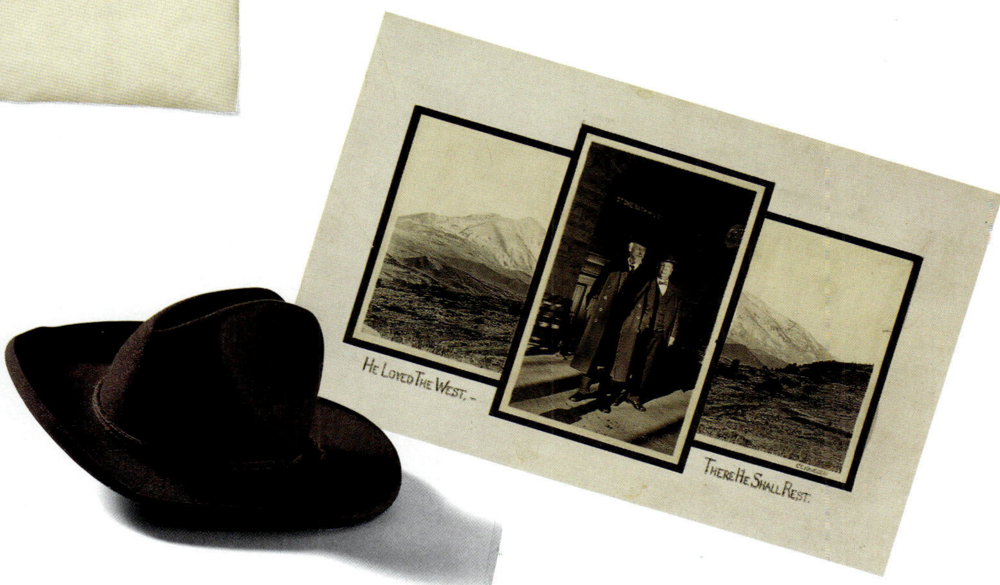

LEFT:
STETSON HAT, C. 1900;
*BUFFALO BILL AND
DR. W. W. CROOK,
GLENWOOD SPRINGS, COLORADO.*
1917. ORIGINAL PHOTOGRAPH.
Shortly before his death in 1917, Buffalo Bill was already planning his next season's tour with the Miller Brothers' 101 Ranch Real Wild West and hoping to finish a series of autobiographical articles he had begun writing. On January 3 he visited Glenwood Springs to recuperate from a severe cold, again fell ill, and returned to Denver, where he died on January 10.

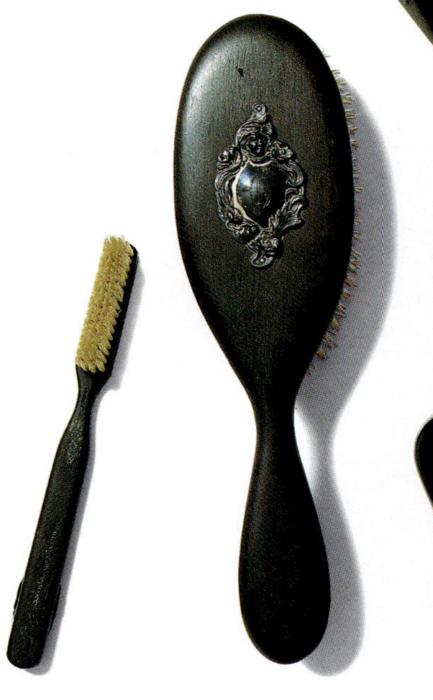

RIGHT:
EBONY GROOMING SET,
MONOGRAMMED "C," C. 1890.
BELONGED TO BUFFALO BILL.

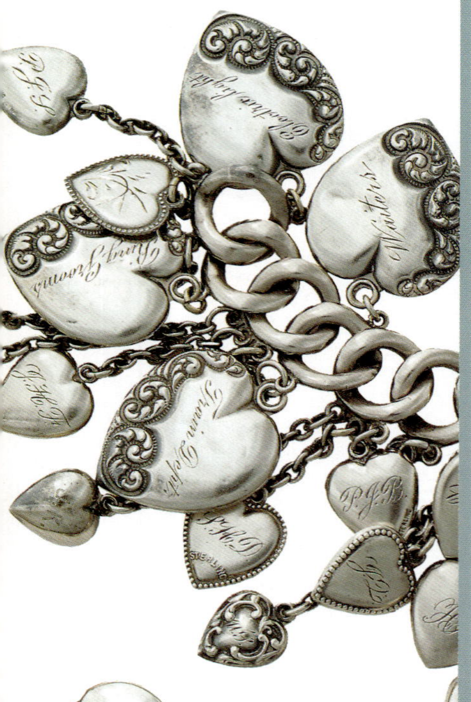

BELOW:
CHARM BRACELET, STERLING SILVER, 1899.
Buffalo Bill's daughters, Arta and Irma, traveled at times with their father in the Wild West show. This bracelet was a gift to Irma from the show's company. Its 67 charms are engraved with performers' names.

BUFFALO BILL AND HIS FAMILY

William F. Cody's parents were descended from American pioneering families. Mary Ann Bonsell Laycock Cody's first American ancestor came to Pennsylvania with William Penn's colony. Isaac Cody was descended from Huguenots (French Protestants) who fled religious persecution and emigrated to Massachusetts in the 1690s.

Will had four sisters—Julia, Eliza, Laura Ella (also known as Helen, or Nellie), and Mary (known as May)—who married and had children. His two brothers, Sam and Charles, died in childhood. An older half-sister, Martha, died in 1858.

Will married Louisa Frederici (1843-1921) in St. Louis in 1866. Her family was from the Alsace region of France. Will and Louisa had four children: Arta Lucille (1866-1904), born at Leavenworth, Kansas; Kit Carson (1870-1876), born at Ft. McPherson, Nebraska; Orra Maude (1872-1883), also born at Ft. McPherson; and Irma Louise (1883-1918), born at North Platte, Nebraska. Irma is buried in Cody; Kit, Orra, and Arta are all buried in Rochester, New York.

Arta and Irma were both married twice, their first husbands suffering untimely deaths. By her first husband, Horton Boal, Arta had two children, Arta Clara and William Cody. Irma had three children by her second husband, Frederick Garlow: Jane, Frederick, Jr., and William.

Buffalo Bill and his sisters have numerous descendants who are among the many family members listed in the directories published by the International Cody Family Association.

RIGHT:
WEDDING DRESS, 1889.
GIFT OF
MR. AND MRS. ROBERT HAYDEN AND
MR. ANTHONY BENN.
Cody's oldest child, Arta, did not live the harsh life of a frontier scout's daughter. She attended a girls' seminary in Rochester, New York, accompanied her father on trips to Italy and England, and wore this silk gown for her marriage to Horton Boal in 1889.

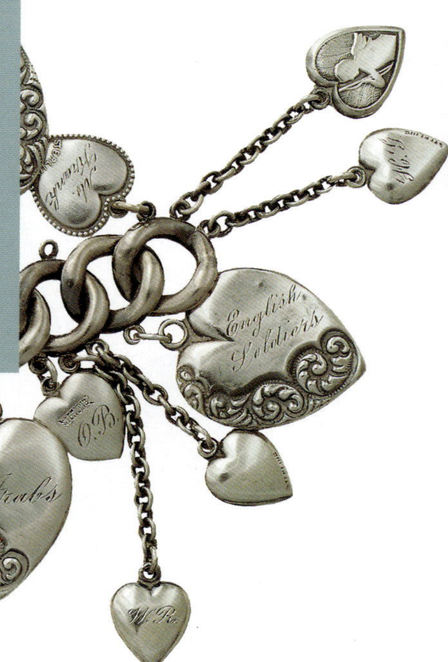

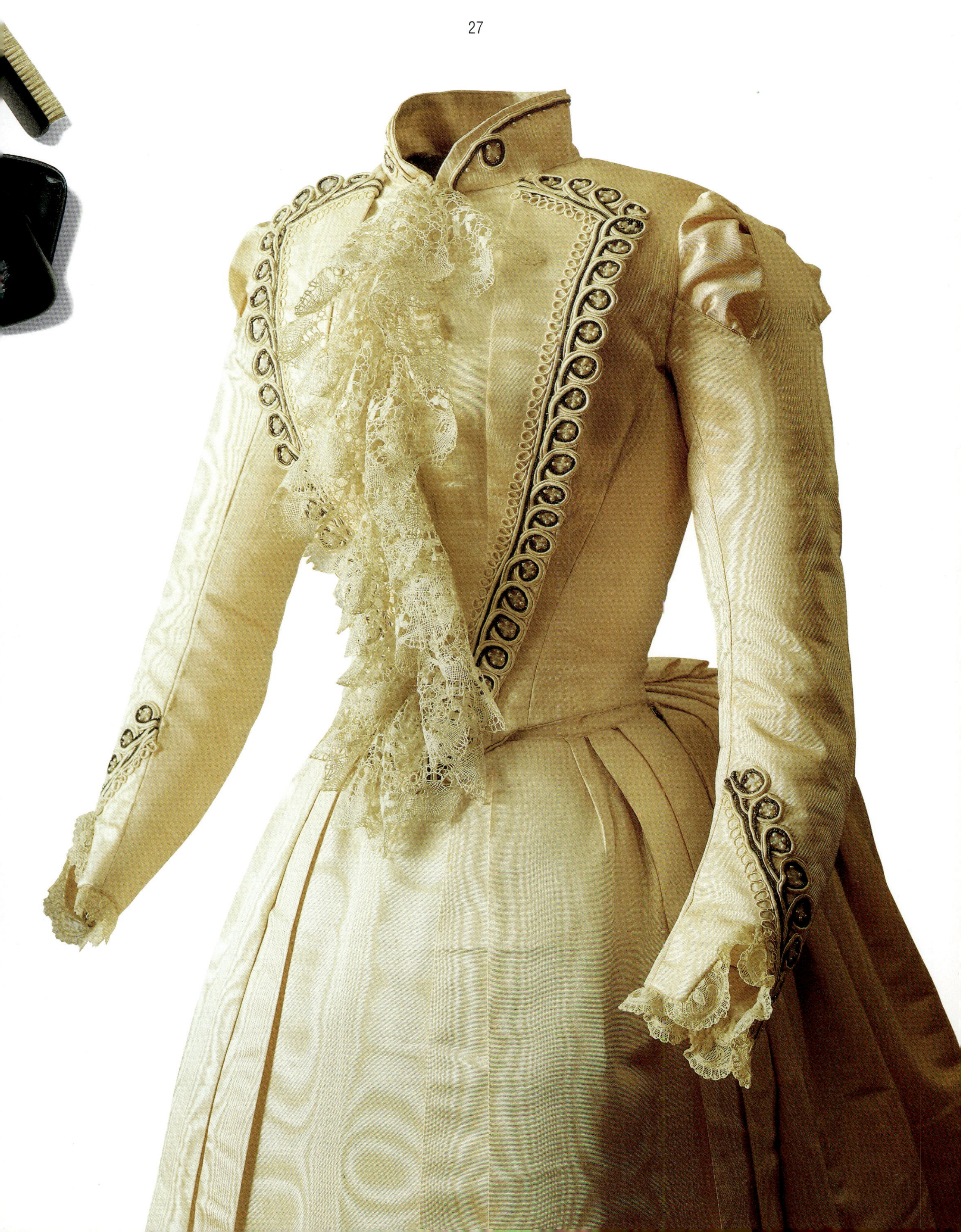

RIGHT:
STOCK CERTIFICATE NO. 1,
BUFFALO BILL'S WILD WEST, 1887.
GIFT OF THE LAW FIRM OF
DEFOREST AND DUER.
Because Buffalo Bill's Wild West represented that part of American life regarded as uniquely American, partners W.F.Cody and Nate Salsbury were invited to take the show to England as part of the U.S. celebration of Queen Victoria's Golden Jubilee. In preparation, Cody and Salsbury along with three other stockholders formed a corporation.

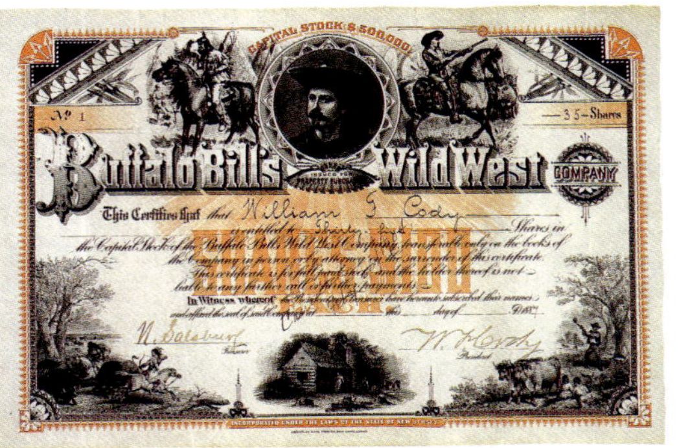

RIGHT:
PORTRAIT OF BUFFALO BILL.
C. 1888. COLOR LITHOGRAPH.
A. HOEN AND CO., LITHOGRAPHERS,
BALTIMORE.
Publicity posters created for the Wild West show were effective works of art. This image asserts Cody's heroic appeal. That he was the main attraction of his own show is apparent.

For 30 years, Buffalo Bill's Wild West show toured the United States and Europe, playing at exhibition grounds to enormous crowds. The scenes and narratives enacted on stage not only defined the quintessential American hero, but also described the basic theme of popular Western history: the contest between nature and civilization, between Indians and whites.

BELOW:
BUFFALO BILL'S WILDER WESTEN,
STUTTGART, GERMANY, 1891.
As a hero to both European and American children, Buffalo Bill appeared in toy sets and in advertising campaigns, on lunch boxes and in picture books like this fold-out edition from Germany published to coincide with the Wild West's 1891 visit.

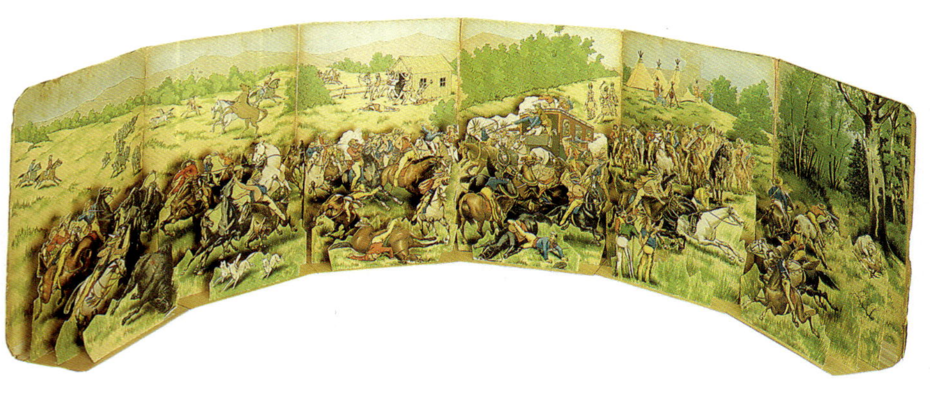

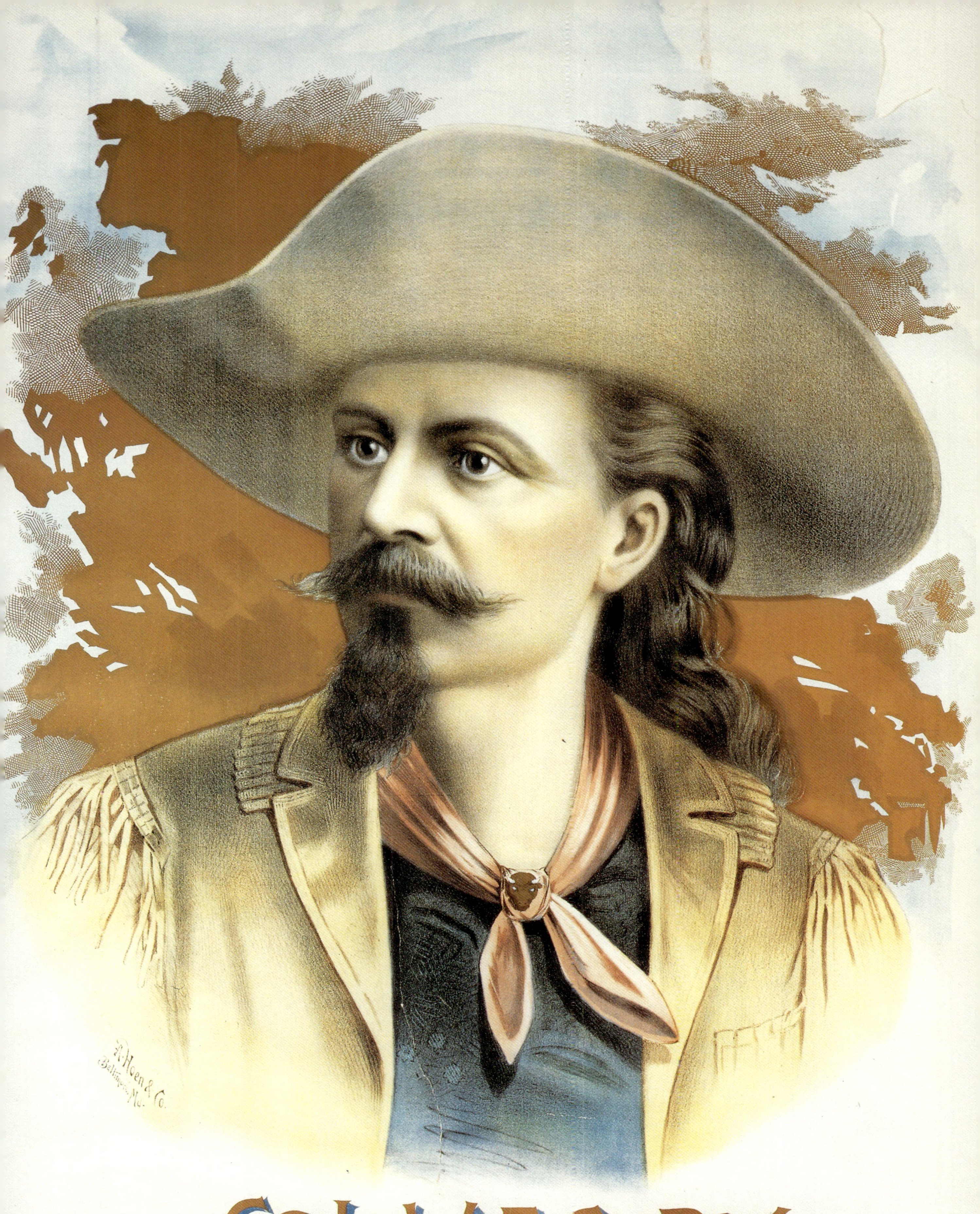

9

BELOW:
WILD WEST SHOW FLAG,
MUSLIN, C. 1885.
Originally numbering in the tens of millions, buffalo symbolized both wildness and progress as they succumbed to pressures from white settlement of the West. They were also closely associated with Buffalo Bill, who estimated that he had shot 4,280 of them to provide meat for crews working for the Kansas Pacific railroad. This flag advertised his show between 1885 and 1910.

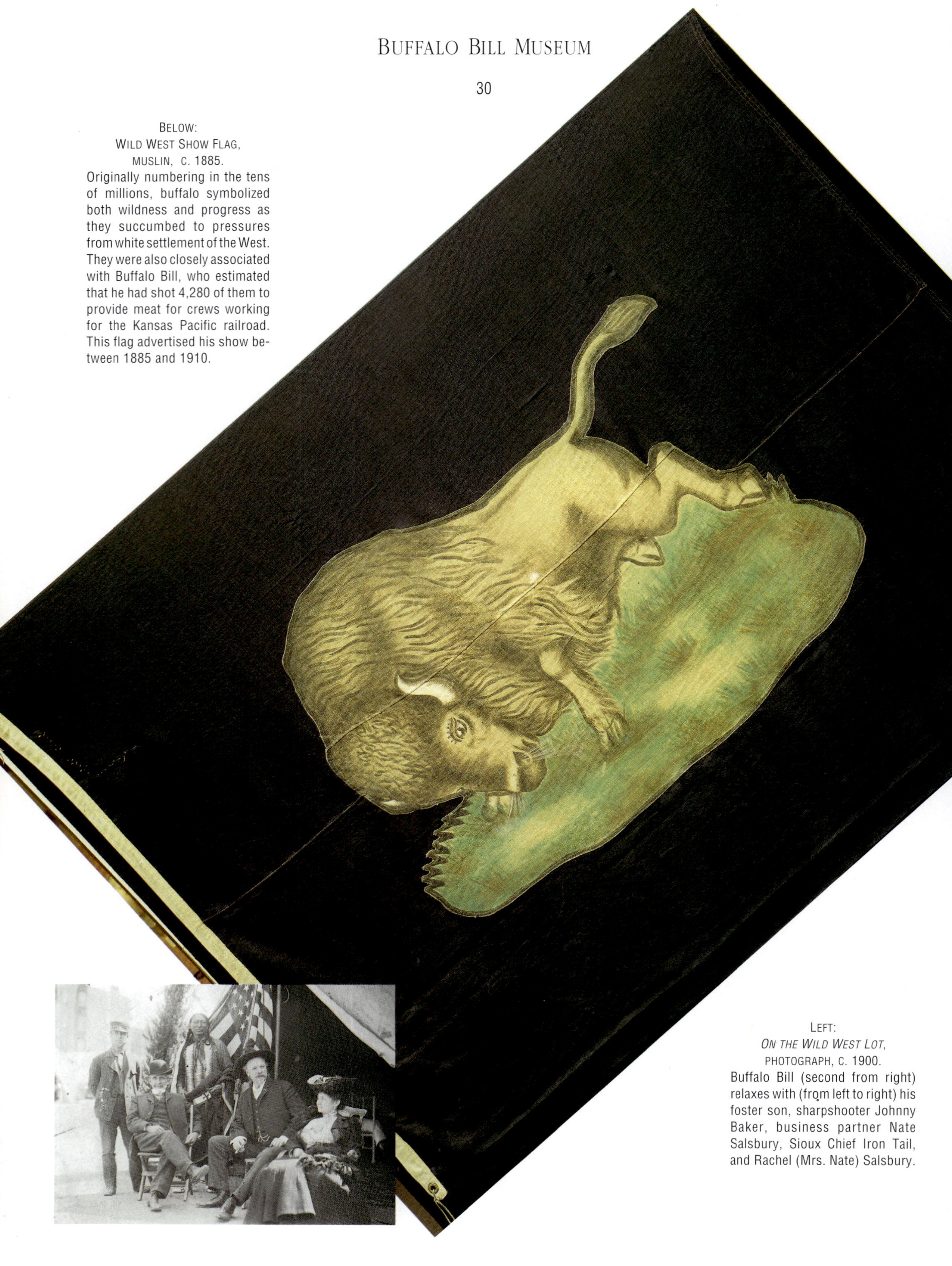

LEFT:
ON THE WILD WEST LOT,
PHOTOGRAPH, C. 1900.
Buffalo Bill (second from right) relaxes with (from left to right) his foster son, sharpshooter Johnny Baker, business partner Nate Salsbury, Sioux Chief Iron Tail, and Rachel (Mrs. Nate) Salsbury.

RIGHT:
SHARPSHOOTERS' TOOLS.
TOP: WINCHESTER MODEL 1894 .32 CALIBER RIFLE ORDERED FOR PRESENTATION TO DOC CARVER BY ZACK MILLER OF THE MILLER BROTHERS' 101 REAL WILD WEST RANCH, 1912. COURTESY OF ARTHUR GOGAN.
MIDDLE: WINCHESTER 1873 .44 CALIBER RIFLE USED BY SHARPSHOOTER AND DIME NOVEL HERO DR. RICHARD "DIAMOND DICK" TANNER. GIFT OF HOWELL HOWARD.
BOTTOM: JOHNNIE BAKER'S WINCHESTER MODEL 1897 16-GAUGE SHOTGUN.

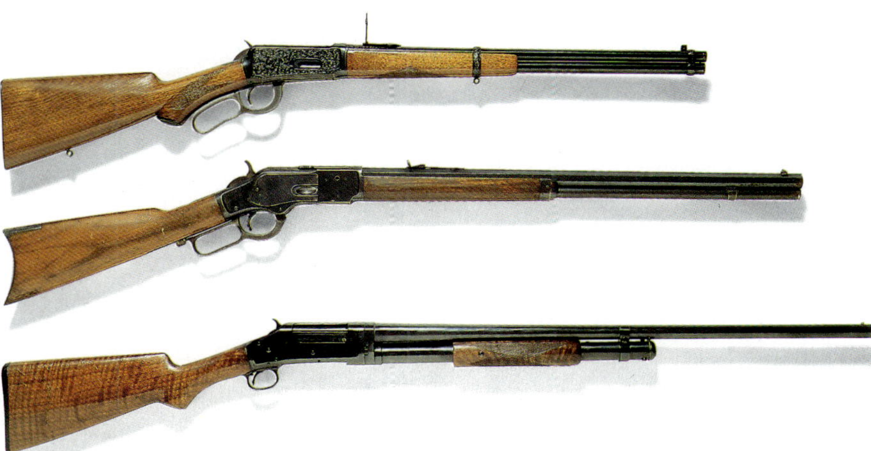

Sharpshooting, horseback riding, roping, shootouts with Indians, harrowing escapes and rescues were all part of the romance audiences had begun to find in Western lore. Buffalo Bill's Wild West drew from this romantic perspective, but supplemented it with the reality Cody knew and personified. At a time when many had started to mourn the passing of the frontier, his dramatic re-enactments of famous incidents and his cast of real-life Westerners were hailed by newspapers as a "living lesson to the youth of the land."

Attending the Wild West show often seemed like an initiation into living history. Spectators visited the tents where performers lived, saw American Indian families relaxing or performing household chores, and watched cowboys and cowgirls tending the show's herds of horses, cattle, and buffalo. If they were lucky, visitors might get an autograph from Cody, Sitting Bull, Annie Oakley or any number of other celebrities. Once the show began, these "heroes" and "villains" recreated actual events and performed feats of genuine skill. Often, visitors themselves participated.

BELOW:
JOHNNIE BAKER, THE MARVELOUS MARKSMAN, 1893.
COLOR LITHOGRAPH.
A. HOEN & COMPANY, BALTIMORE.
Performer and arena director, Lewis H. "Johnnie" Baker (1869-1931) first appeared in the Wild West show as a teenager. Raised on a Nebraska ranch, he was billed as "The Cowboy Kid."

BELOW:
DOC CARVER'S SADDLE, C. 1884.
GIFT OF HOWELL HOWARD.
Cody's erstwhile business partner, a man he described as having gone "west on a piano stool," Dr. W. F. Carver (1840-1927) was a notable marksman and hunter, though not the frontiersman he claimed to be. This famous saddle is decorated with coins he shot during his arena act.

BELOW:
JOHNNIE BAKER'S STETSON HAT, WHITE FELT WITH GROSGRAIN BAND AND TRIM, C. 1920.
As a neighbor of the Codys, Baker had grown up admiring Buffalo Bill; most of his adult life was spent working for him as a performer or manager. He later started the Buffalo Bill Memorial Museum on Lookout Mountain, Colorado.

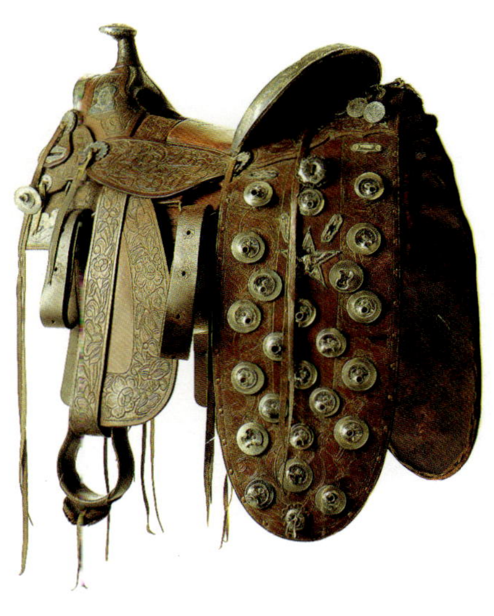

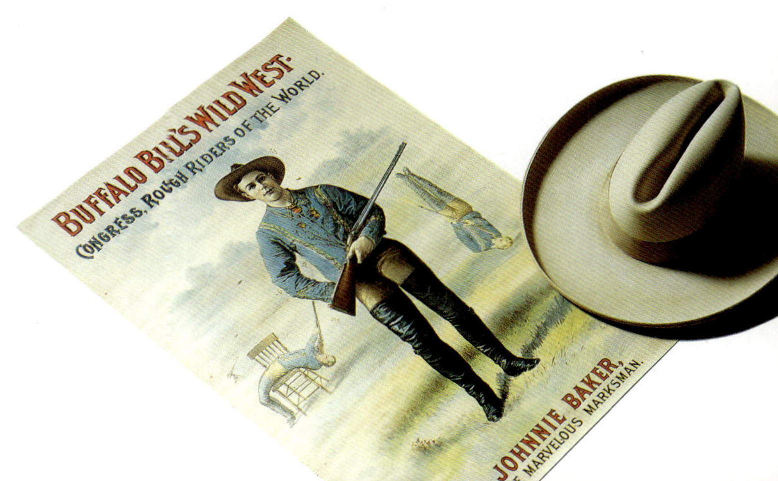

RIGHT:
COLT MODEL 1873 SINGLE-ACTION REVOLVER, .45 CALIBER, 1900.
GIFT OF LILLIAN BURCH THOMPSON;
AND FORRESTER SINGLE-SHOT PISTOL, C. 1880.
GIFT OF BLANCHE CARVER LEWIS, NIECE OF W.F. CARVER.
Doc Carver owned and used this Forrester target pistol (top); the Colt (below) belonged to chief cowboy George W. Burch.

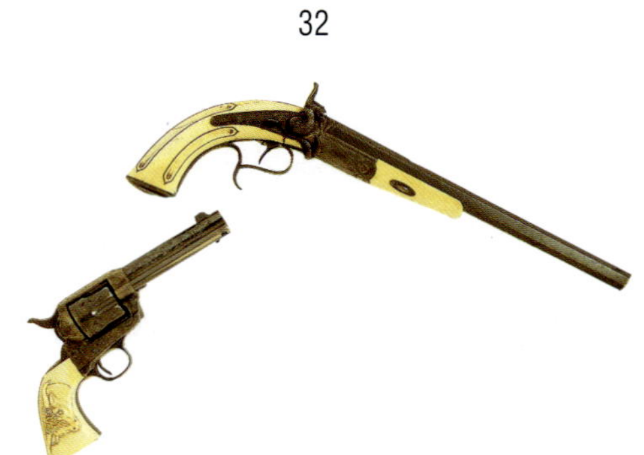

RIGHT:
BUFFALO BILL AND THE MILLER BROTHERS' 101 RANCH,
CHICAGO 1916.
ORIGINAL PHOTOGRAPH.
After the Wild West folded in 1913, Cody toured with the Sells-Floto Circus. His 1916 stint with the Miller Brothers' 101 Ranch Real Wild West was more enjoyable, and paid about the same—$100 a day, plus a share of the profits.

One of the show's most popular skits—"Attack on the Deadwood Stage Coach"—involved not only watching the anticipated cowboys and Indians duke it out in the arena, but also called for volunteers from the audience. Following an introduction that solemnly warned of impending danger, the driver of the stage and his volunteer passengers found themselves under attack by Indian raiders. The driver tried to outrun the warriors, then outshoot them; finally, Buffalo Bill arrived to save the day. The dust, screams, gunshots, war cries, smoke and confusion left participants thrilled and confident that they had just replayed a scene right out of Buffalo Bill's life.

Over the years, Cody added new versions of his classic shoot-'em-up. "Attack on a Settler's Cabin," "Holiday at the TE Ranch," the "Great Hold-Up" and "Bandit Hunters of the Union Pacific," and "Attack on an Emigrant Train" were all variations on the theme, though the imitations never matched the excitement and popularity of the original.

"Rough riding" was also central to the Wild West show. Riders included American Indians, white cowboys and cowgirls, and Mexican vaqueros, all competing in races against each other. Over time, the "congress" of skilled equestrians counted as members Russian Cossacks, gauchos from Argentina, Syrians, Arabs, Cubans, Japanese "samurai," Boers and Hawaiians. Cavalry drills were also popular, using detachments from top-notch units of the United States, Great Britain, Germany and France.

There were many other mounted events—bareback and relay races; daring "Pony Express" rides; square dances; a "Gymkana" that required riders to perform a series of maneuvers including dismounting, lighting a cigar, opening an umbrella, and remounting with cigar and umbrella in hand.

FAR RIGHT:
STAGECOACH,
ABBOTT DOWNING CO.,
CONCORD, NEW HAMPSHIRE, 1867.
GIFT OF OLIVE AND GLENN NIELSON.
Purchased by Buffalo Bill's Wild West in 1911, this coach was used for the perennially popular "Attack on the Deadwood Stage Coach." Cody had acquired his first coach in 1883 from the Cheyenne and Black Hills stage line for $1,800.

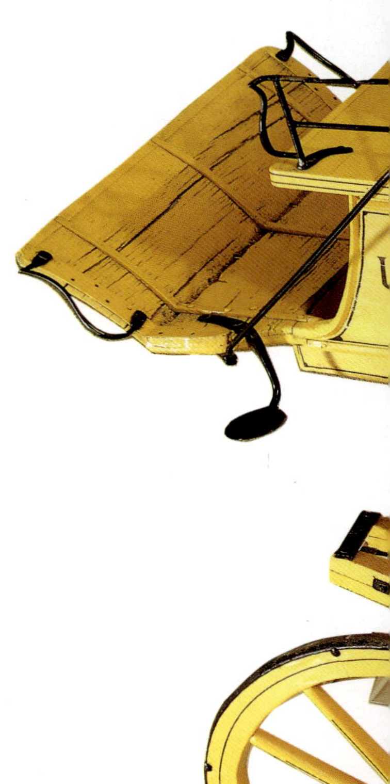

BELOW:
PAWNEE BILL AND BUFFALO BILL,
ORIGINAL PHOTOGRAPH,
AUTOGRAPHED 1910.
Gordon William Lillie (1860-1942) earned the nickname "Pawnee Bill" as an interpreter at the Pawnee Agency, Oklahoma. After organizing his own outdoor exhibitions, he became Cody's partner in 1908 in the combined Buffalo Bill's Wild West and Pawnee Bill's Far East.

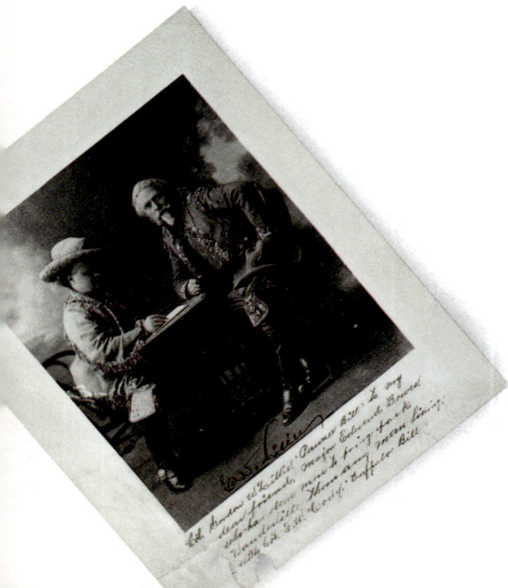

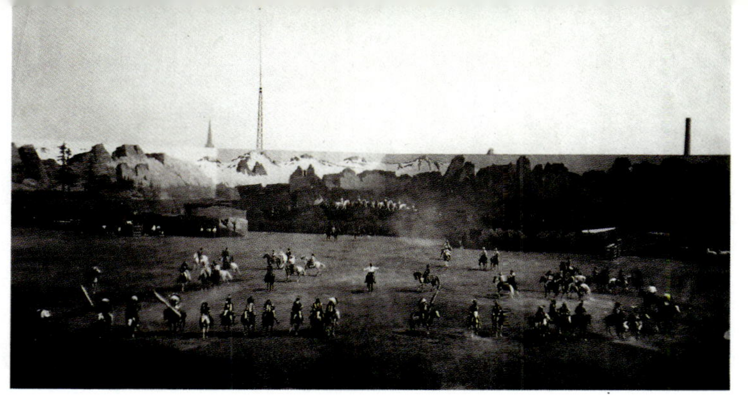

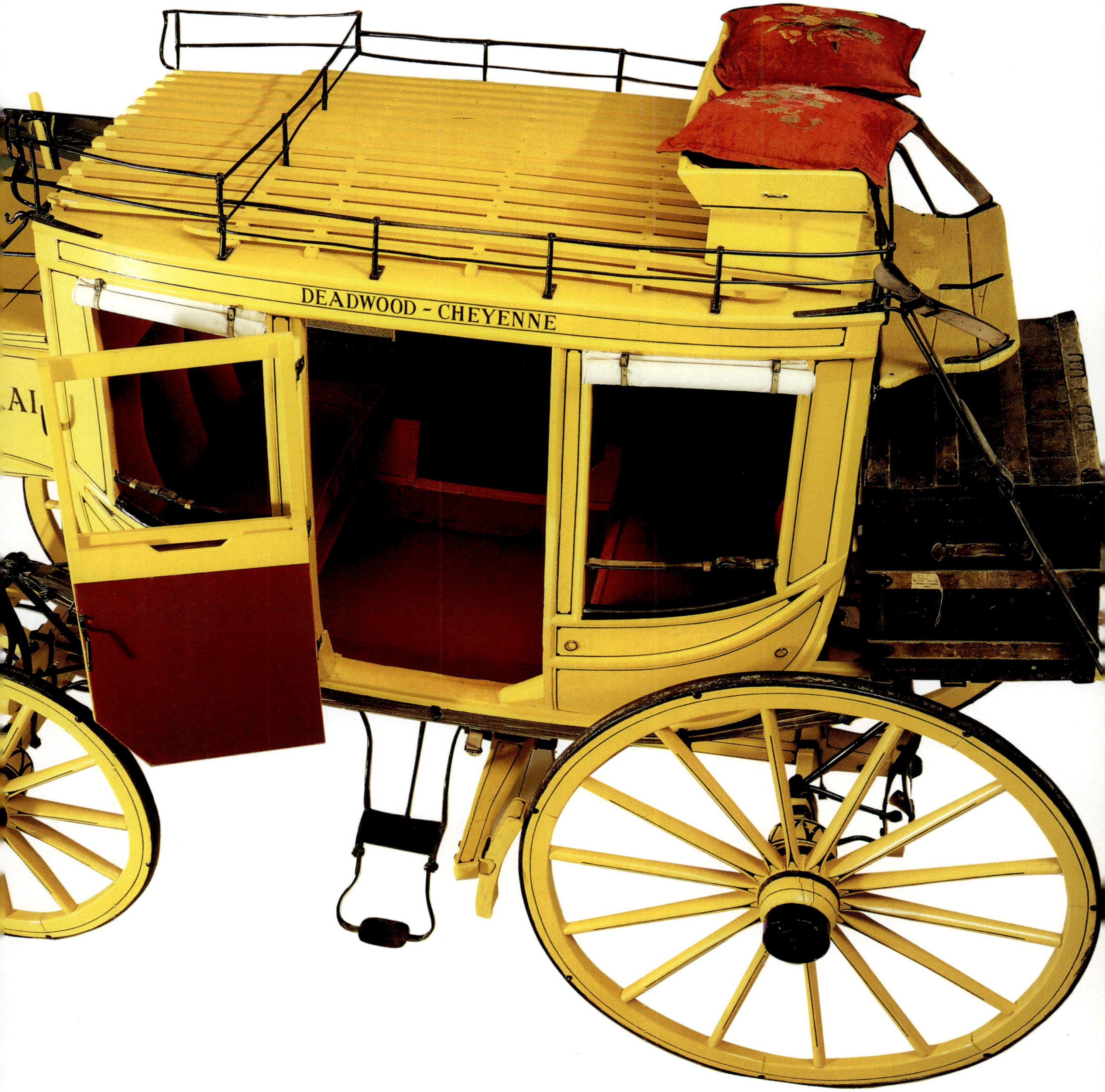

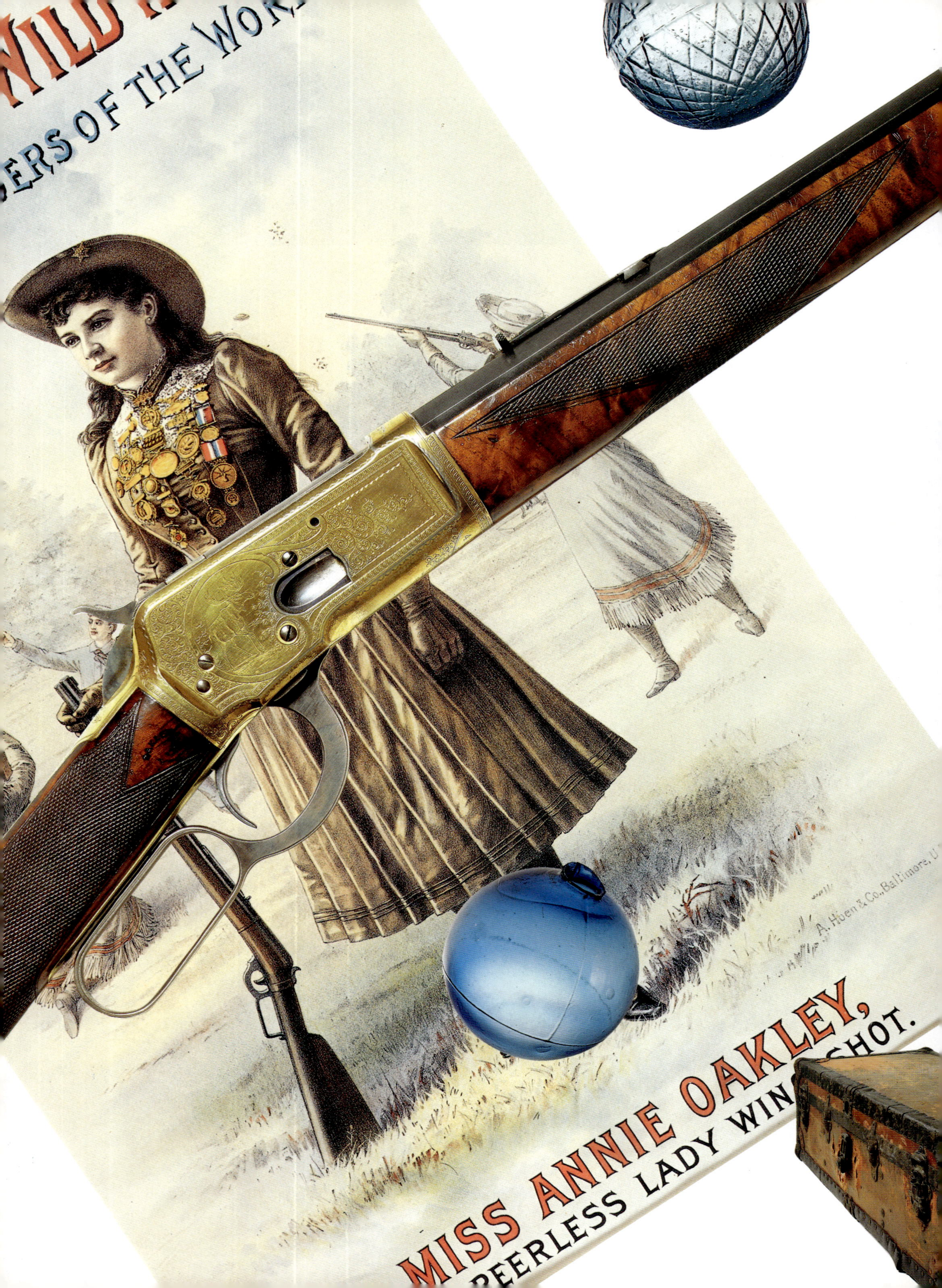

MISS ANNIE OAKLEY,
A. Hoen & Co., Baltimore

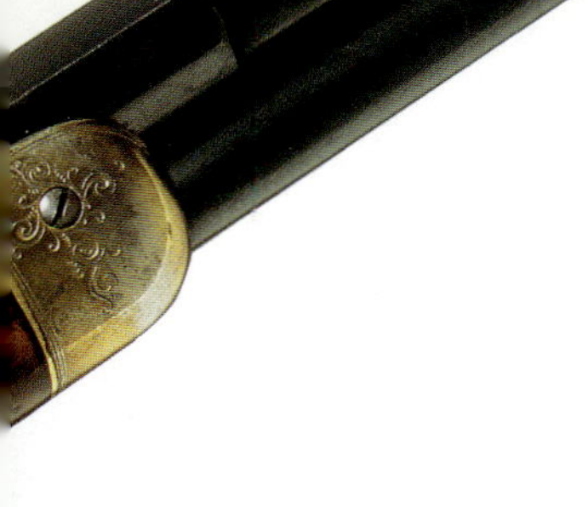

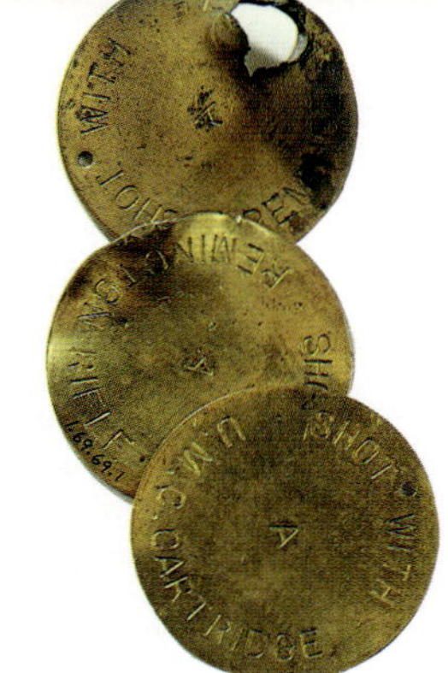

RIGHT:
BRASS TARGETS, C. 1901.
Annie Oakley and Frank Butler performed shooting demonstrations for the UMC Company using these half-dollar-sized targets. Though Annie Oakley's skill was undeniable, her attractiveness and small stature were also highlighted in posters and brochures.

LEFT:
ANNIE OAKLEY, PEERLESS LADY WINGSHOT, 1893.
COLOR LITHOGRAPH.
A. HOEN & CO., BALTIMORE.
GIFT OF THE COE FOUNDATION.
Called "Little Sure Shot" by Sioux leader Sitting Bull and "Missie" by Buffalo Bill, Annie Oakley (1860-1926) was a star performer for 17 years, and the Wild West show's first woman employee. Born Phoebe Ann Moses in Darke County, Ohio, she learned to shoot wild game to provide for her family.

LEFT:
ANNIE OAKLEY'S WINCHESTER MODEL 1892 RIFLE, .32 CALIBER, GOLD PLATED AND ENGRAVED.
GIFT OF SPENCER OLIN.
This rifle was custom-made for Annie Oakley and decorated by master-engraver John Ulrich in 1895.

Men and women showed off during the "Cowboy Fun" acts. They rode broncs, lassoed wild horses, herded cattle, rode bareback, grabbed handkerchiefs from the ground while galloping by, and generally risked breaking their necks. During the years the show toured Europe, performers often challenged local horsemen to ride a prairie bronc or were themselves challenged to tame a European horse in friendly competitions that pitted Western skill against European tradition.

Sharpshooting was a particularly spectacular part of the show. Until his later years, Buffalo Bill saddled up to exhibit his marksmanship, shattering glass target balls thrown into the air while he rode at a full gallop. A sharpshooting farm boy from North Platte, Nebraska, Johnnie Baker—the "Cowboy Kid"—showed how he could stand on his head and maintain perfect aim. And of course there was Annie Oakley, whose act always immediately followed the opening Grand Processional. Oakley skipped girlishly into the arena, shot coins from the hands of her husband and manager, Frank Butler, and charmed audiences with her eagle eye and feminine poise.

Although American Indians in the Wild West usually played obstacles to white expansion, they received fair pay and fair treatment as employees of Buffalo Bill. Despite depicting painful events in their tribal histories, most Native Americans performers and their families found life on tour preferable to life on the reservation. Also, the show provided one of the first opportunities for white Europeans and Americans to interact with Indian people. If it depicted stereotypical mounted plains warriors, the show also defined them as brave and dashing—suitable antagonists for Buffalo Bill.

LEFT:
GLASS TARGET BALLS, C. 1890.
GIFT OF ALEX KERR.
Introduced to the United States in the 1850s, glass targets did not become popular until Wild West performer Captain A. H. Bogardus designed a workable glass target launcher in 1877 that made them simulate the flight of passenger pigeons, a favorite target for competitive shooting.

LOWER LEFT:
FOOTLOCKER, WOOD AND LEATHER WITH BRASS CLOSURES AND CORNER TABS, STENCILED "ANNIE OAKLEY," C. 1890.
ARNOTT MILLETT COLLECTION.
GIFT OF WILLIAM SELF.
Annie Oakley and her husband, Frank Butler, toured as a duo until Annie was hired by Buffalo Bill in 1885, with Frank as her manager. Their marriage endured 50 years of travel and public scrutiny.

BELOW:
ANNIE OAKLEY'S SADDLE,
COLLINS & MORRISON, C. 1893.
An accomplished rider, Annie Oakley often performed in the saddle. Note the hand grips on the swell for trick riding.

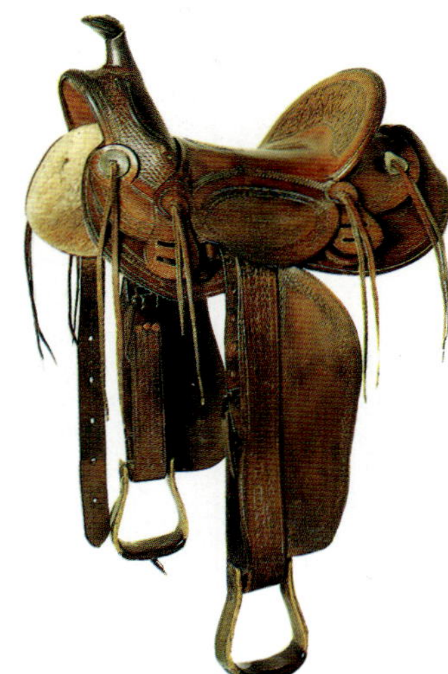

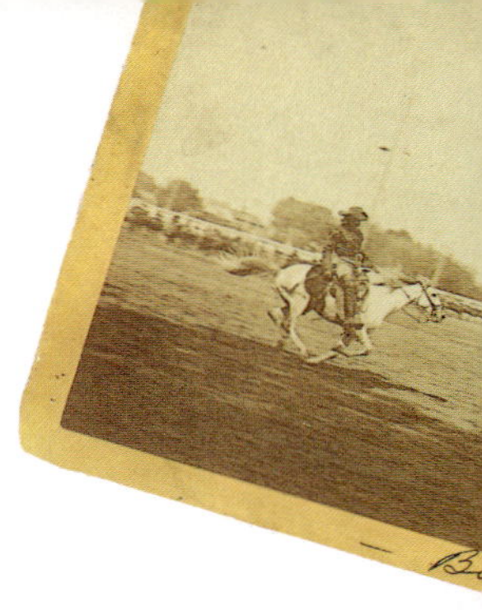

RIGHT:
COSSACK SHASHQA (SABER) AND KINDJAL (DAGGER), C. 1895.
Cossacks toured with the Wild West show as part of the Congress of Rough Riders of the World. Their act included stunt riding and "Native Dance." Billed as "the flower" of the various "hordes" that roamed Asia's steppes, they were much admired by Queen Victoria.

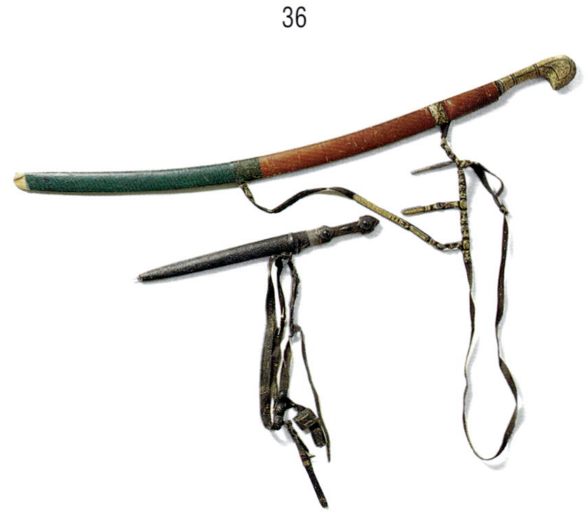

Because military conflict continued to be a major emphasis of popular Western lore, Cody drew on some of his own famous exploits. The re-enactment of his 1876 duel with Yellow Hair in particular pleased the crowds, and it remained on the show's program for many years. Custer's defeat at the Little Bighorn was another favorite attraction, complete with its invented ending—Buffalo Bill riding through the corpse-strewn battlefield as the words "Too Late" appeared on a screen behind him.

Continuing his self-appointed role as spokesman for the Army and military "preparedness," Cody incorporated contemporary battle scenes into the show. The Battle of Tien-Tsin from the Boxer Rebellion in China and battles from the Boer Wars in South Africa were re-enacted before the crowds. When outdoorsman and Rough Rider Theodore Roosevelt emerged as a hero in the United States during the Spanish-American War, his exploits at the Battle of San Juan Hill were reinterpreted by Buffalo Bill's Wild West.

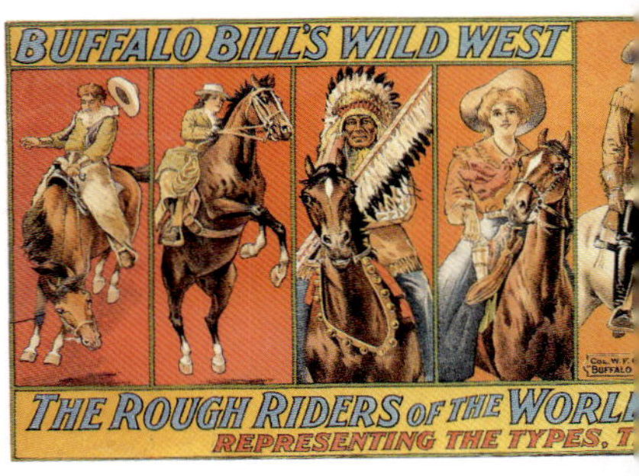

ABOVE:
BUFFALO BILL'S WILD WEST. 1910.
LITHOGRAPH. U.S. LITHO
RUSSELL-MORGAN PRINT, CINCINNATI.
GIFT OF CARL DOWNING.
Called a "Babel of tongues" by one reporter, the Wild West show's backlot featured a multicultural company including riders from five continents and diverse ethnic groups.

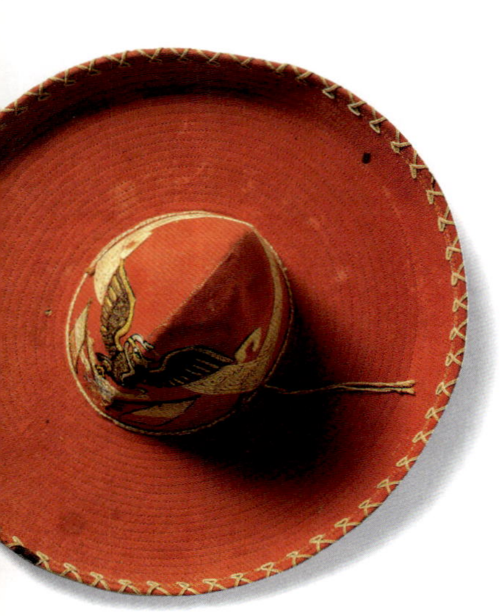

ABOVE:
SOMBRERO, RED FELT WITH EAGLE EMBROIDERY, C. 1900.
GIFT OF IRVING H. "LARRY" LAROM ESTATE.
The cowboy's outfit derived from the flamboyant yet practical gear of the vaqueros of Mexico. It was through Buffalo Bill's and later Wild West shows, and the illustrations of Frederic Remington and other artists, that the public in the 1880s began to identify the outfit as the occupational uniform of the cowboy.

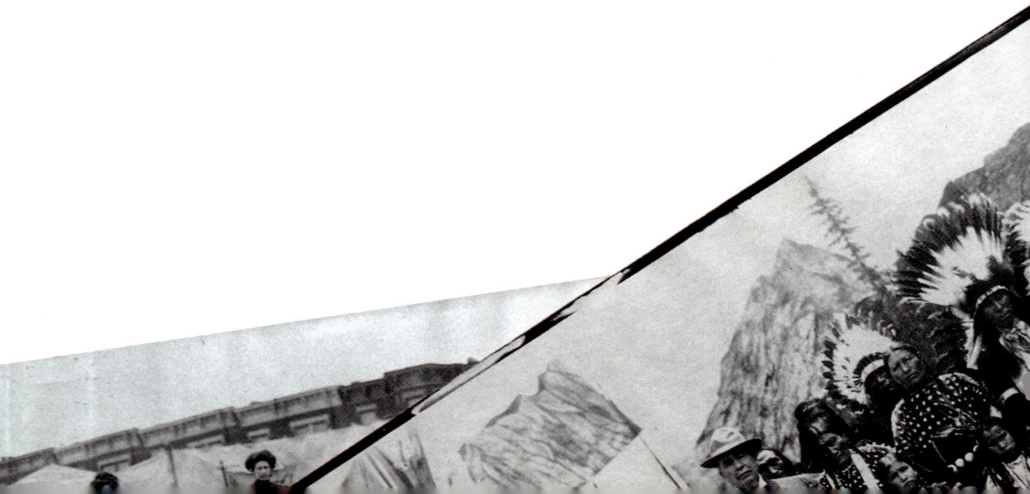

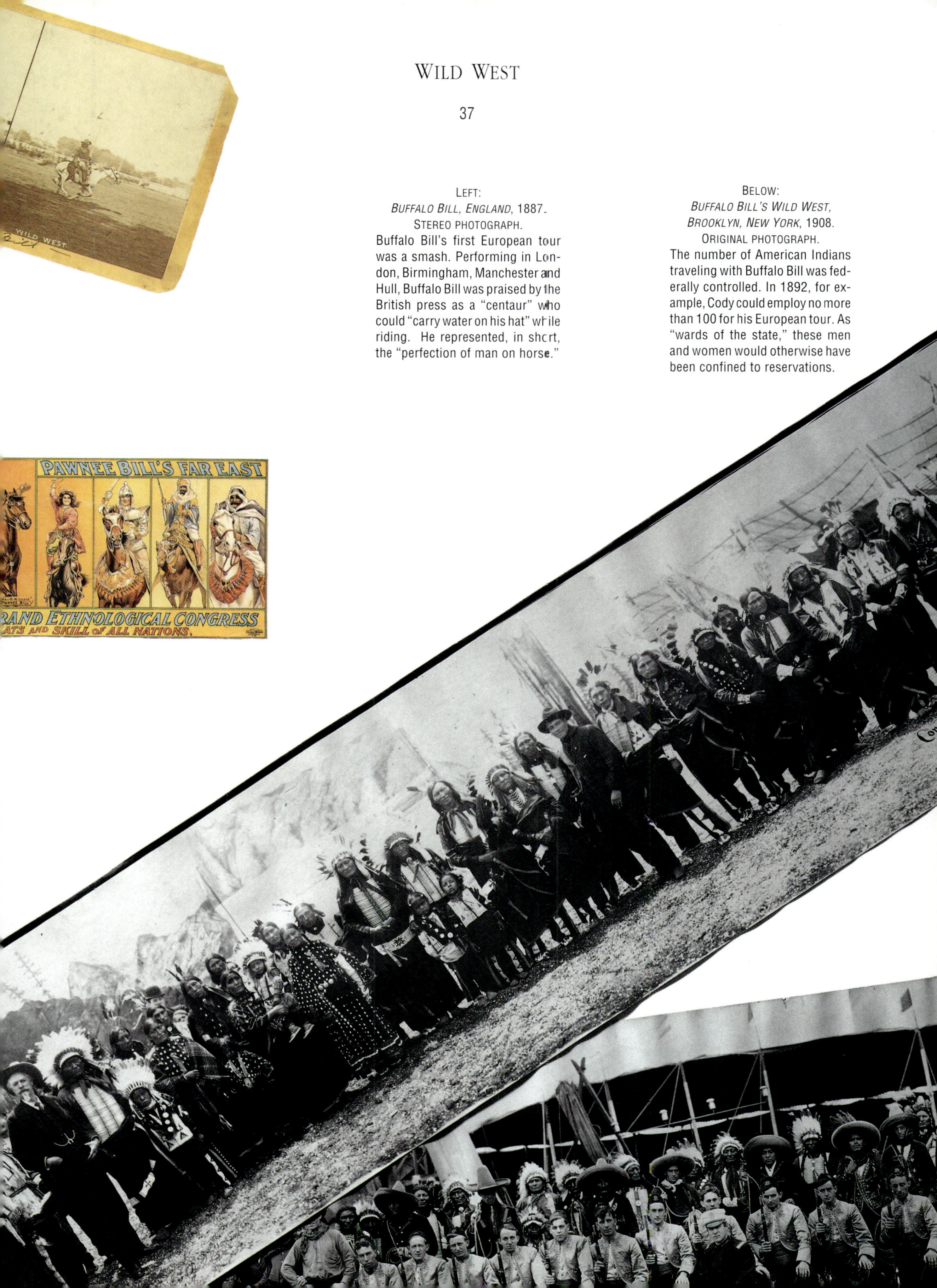

LEFT:
BUFFALO BILL, ENGLAND, 1887.
STEREO PHOTOGRAPH.
Buffalo Bill's first European tour was a smash. Performing in London, Birmingham, Manchester and Hull, Buffalo Bill was praised by the British press as a "centaur" who could "carry water on his hat" while riding. He represented, in short, the "perfection of man on horse."

BELOW:
BUFFALO BILL'S WILD WEST, BROOKLYN, NEW YORK, 1908.
ORIGINAL PHOTOGRAPH.
The number of American Indians traveling with Buffalo Bill was federally controlled. In 1892, for example, Cody could employ no more than 100 for his European tour. As "wards of the state," these men and women would otherwise have been confined to reservations.

BELOW:
MONOGRAMMED RING, 1890.
This gold and enameled-silver ring set with diamonds was given to William Cody by Luitpold Ludwig, Prince Regent of Bavaria. The Wild West show's European appearances were well-attended by royalty. They almost universally admired Buffalo Bill as one of "Nature's Noblemen."

LEFT:
MONOGRAMMED STICKPIN,
GOLD WITH DIAMONDS, 1902.
This stickpin was a gift to Cody from Edward VII, crowned King of England in 1901 following the death of his mother, Queen Victoria. As Prince of Wales he had attended the 1887 Wild West show, where he and Cody had become mutual admirers. As monarch, he made time to see the 1902-1903 show three weeks before it closed.

BELOW:
GOLD WATCH,
MONOGRAM IN DIAMONDS, 1890.
Victor Emmanuel III, crowned King of Italy in 1900, presented this watch to Cody in 1890 during the Wild West's Italian tour.

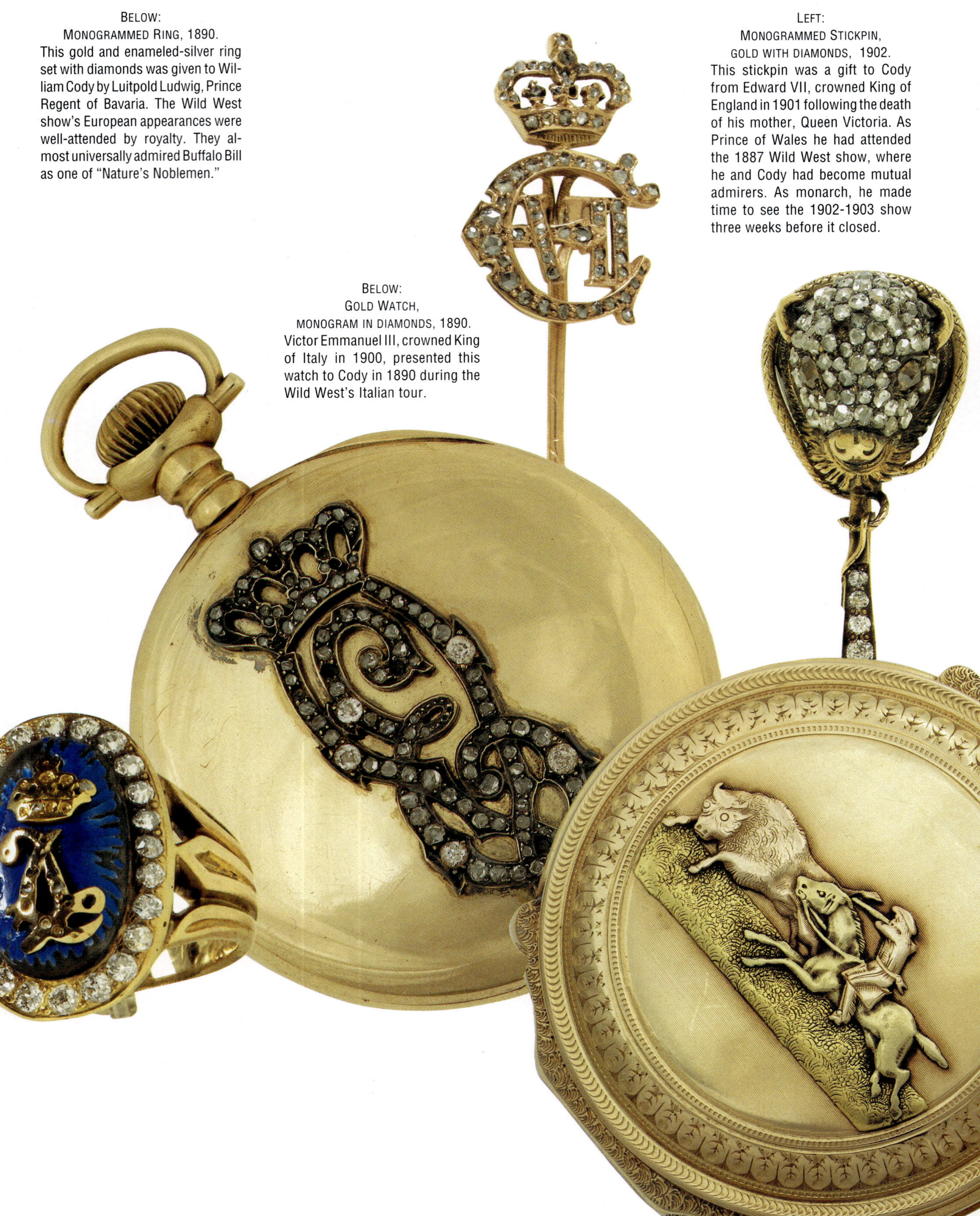

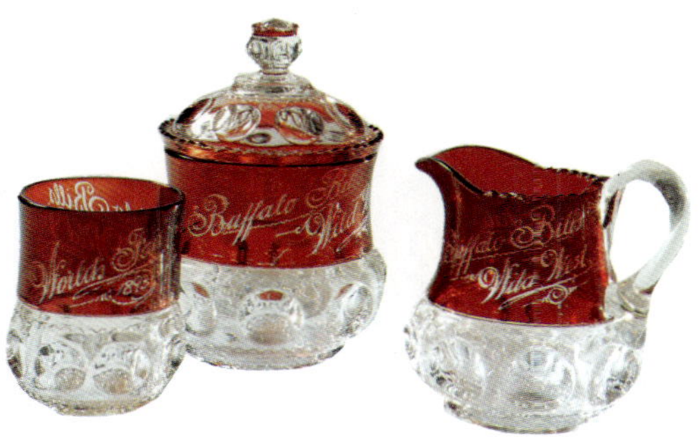

RIGHT:
RUBY PRESSED GLASSWARE, 1893.
This glassware was a souvenir of the Wild West show's appearance at the Chicago World's Fair. Buffalo Bill's Wild West in 1893 put together one of the most successful years ever in outdoor show business history.

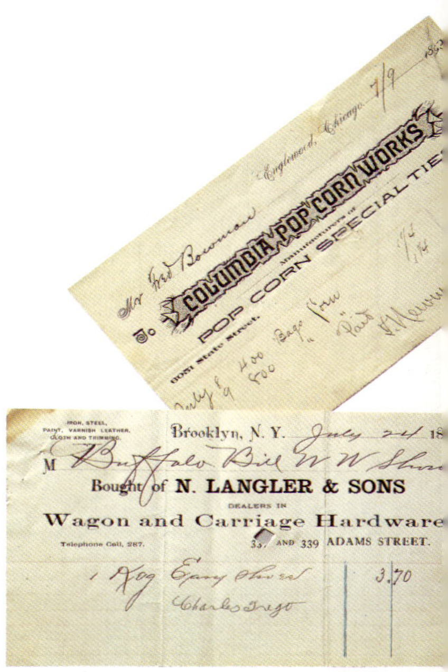

COLUMBIA POP CORN WORKS
POP CORN SPECIALTIE

Brooklyn, N. Y.
Bought of N. LANGLER & SONS
DEALERS IN
Wagon and Carriage Hardware
AND 339 ADAMS STREET.

BELOW:
INVOICES TO THE WILD WEST SHOW, 1893 AND 1894.
The logistics of the Wild West were formidable. Cody and Salsbury were so adept at transporting equipment, livestock, and personnel that Kaiser Wilhelm assigned special agents to study their methods.

LEFT:
TIE PIN, GOLD WITH DIAMONDS AND RUBIES, 1872.
Grand Duke Alexis presented Cody with this pin following his scouting efforts during the Royal Buffalo Hunt of 1872. The buffalo head is formed by diamonds, with rubies for the eyes.

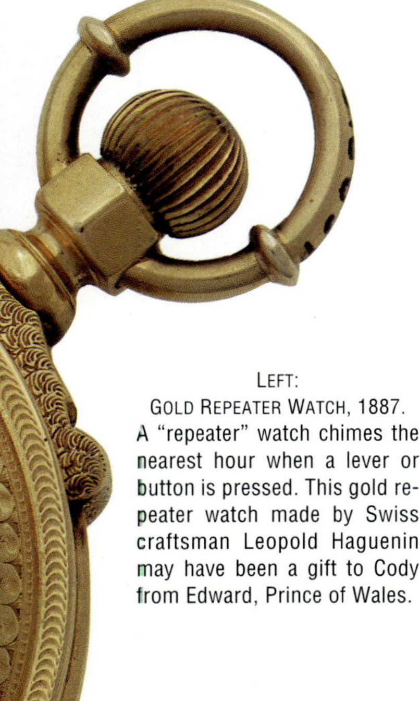

LEFT:
GOLD REPEATER WATCH, 1887.
A "repeater" watch chimes the nearest hour when a lever or button is pressed. This gold repeater watch made by Swiss craftsman Leopold Haguenin may have been a gift to Cody from Edward, Prince of Wales.

Audiences responded to Cody's innovations. Like contemporary documentaries, Wild West show performances seemed timely as well as entertaining. Couriers, heralds and other advertising brochures produced for Cody and his press agent, John Burke, contained dramatic illustrations and stories that appealed to children and adults. As the *Illinois State Journal* pointed out in 1883, the frontier as depicted in the Wild West show was "of the very highest importance to children, because by the time they are adults the whole thing will have gone to the forgotten past." The capturing of a passing world and of vanishing cultures was deemed one of Cody's most important legacies to American boys and girls.

But schoolchildren were not the only ones to get the message. Buffalo Bill's Wild West spent a total of 10 years and six tours in Europe, making an impact on commoner and royalty alike. In fact, Europeans would long accept the show as the definitive source for Western American fact and fiction.

Though ocean crossings were difficult and seasickness commonplace, the company found financial and public relations bonanzas in England, France and Italy. It was not uncommon for kings, princes, dukes, visiting sheiks and African royalty to ride in the Deadwood Stage Coach or present Cody with jewelry, watches and other tokens of esteem. Colorful posters and exuberant press releases in Paris, Milan or Cologne heralded the imminent arrival of Buffalo Bill's Wild West. It is no overstatement that at the turn of the century, Buffalo Bill Cody was the most famous American in the world.

BELOW:
NATE SALSBURY'S DESK, MAHOGANY, C. 1898.
GIFT OF MR. WARREN JAMES OAKES, GRANDSON OF NATE SALSBURY.
Nate Salsbury (1846-1902) was a theater veteran when he became Buffalo Bill's partner in 1883. His business acumen benefitted the show. Though he resented Cody's prominence, he remained Cody's partner until his death.

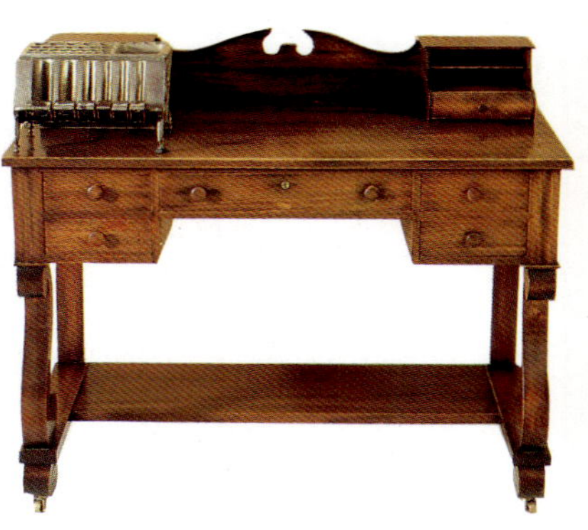

RIGHT:
MANTEL CLOCK ORNAMENT,
BRONZE-COLORED ZINC ALLOY,
C. 1900.
Ornaments sold by catalogue beginning in about 1890 coincided with Buffalo Bill's increasing fame and popularity. The horseman may have been a generic "cavalier" figurine, but with the addition of a lasso and a Stetson, it became Buffalo Bill.

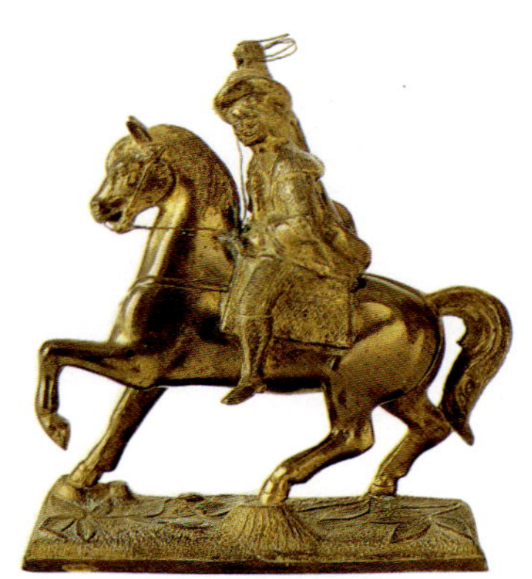

RIGHT:
FILM
Buffalo Bill moved easily from the arena to film making. He oversaw the making and theatrical release of motion pictures of Buffalo Bill's Wild West and of a feature film, *The Indian Wars*.

FAR RIGHT:
BUFFALO BILL AND PAWNEE BILL,
1911. COLOR LITHOGRAPH.
ADOLPH FRIEDLANDER,
HAMBURG, GERMANY.
The Wild West show's Far East component enacted "a dream of the Orient" using camels, elephants, whirling dervishes and Bedouins, with Polynesians and boomerang throwers for real exotic flavor. This poster advertised the European release of a film of the Wild West.

FAR RIGHT:
BUCKSKIN JACKET, C.1910.
GIFT OF
MR. AND MRS. JEFF ANDERSON.
This bead-trimmed jacket was owned and worn by Gordon W. Lillie, Pawnee Bill. His wife, Smith College graduate May Manning Lillie, whom he met in Philadelphia in 1886, learned marksmanship and became a featured Wild West sharpshooter.

For 20 years, the Wild West show thrived. Cody and his partner, Nate Salsbury, scheduled an unprecedented run of successful tours and appearances. But as the 1900s progressed, outdoor dramas had to compete with new entertainments, including motion pictures. Following Salsbury's death, Cody and his new partner, Pawnee Bill Lillie, created the combined Buffalo Bill's Wild West and Pawnee Bill's Far East. Though they made film versions of the show, attendance declined, and, deep in financial trouble, they declared bankruptcy in 1913. Later that same year, Cody produced a five-reel recreation of the Battle of Wounded Knee and other Indian Wars conflicts featuring many of the original participants. He toured with other shows—Sells-Floto Circus and Miller Brothers 101 Ranch—and was planning future projects at the time of his death in 1917.

Looking back from the other end of a violent and chaotic century, our society has become a cynical judge of the world that preceded our own time. But no matter how contemporary scholars see his life, the fact remains that Buffalo Bill was more than a showman. He hunted buffalo for the railroad, rode for the Pony Express and scouted for the U.S. Army. Now he is remembered almost exclusively for describing a rowdy and colorful frontier that still echoes in our history, art and politics, but once his fame rested on an indivisible combination of authenticity and romance.

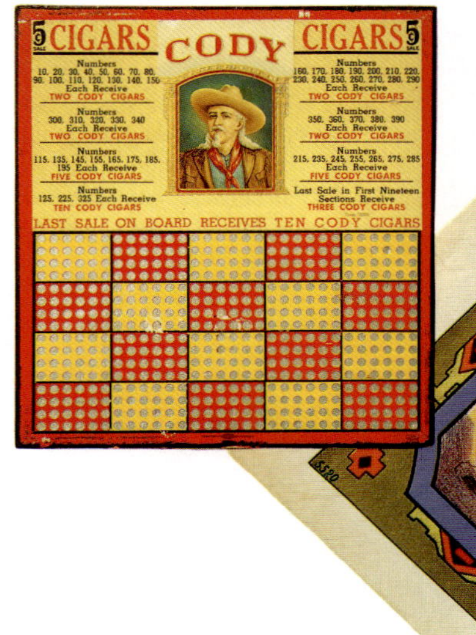

ABOVE:
PUNCH BOARD GAMBLING GAME,
C. 1930. GIFT OF HUGH MCLEAN.
Buffalo Bill's image has been used to advertise many products not only during his lifetime but to the present day.

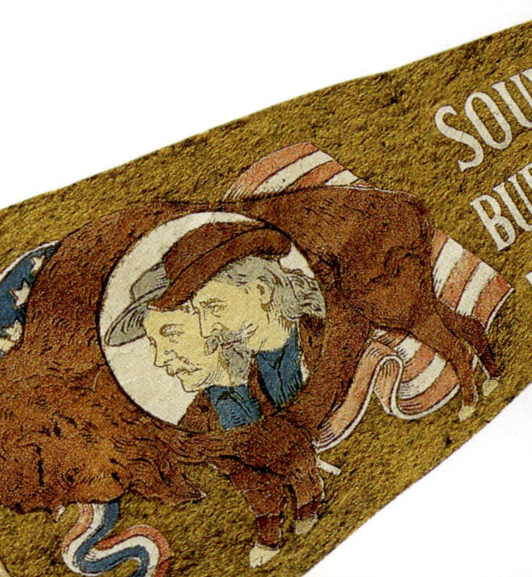

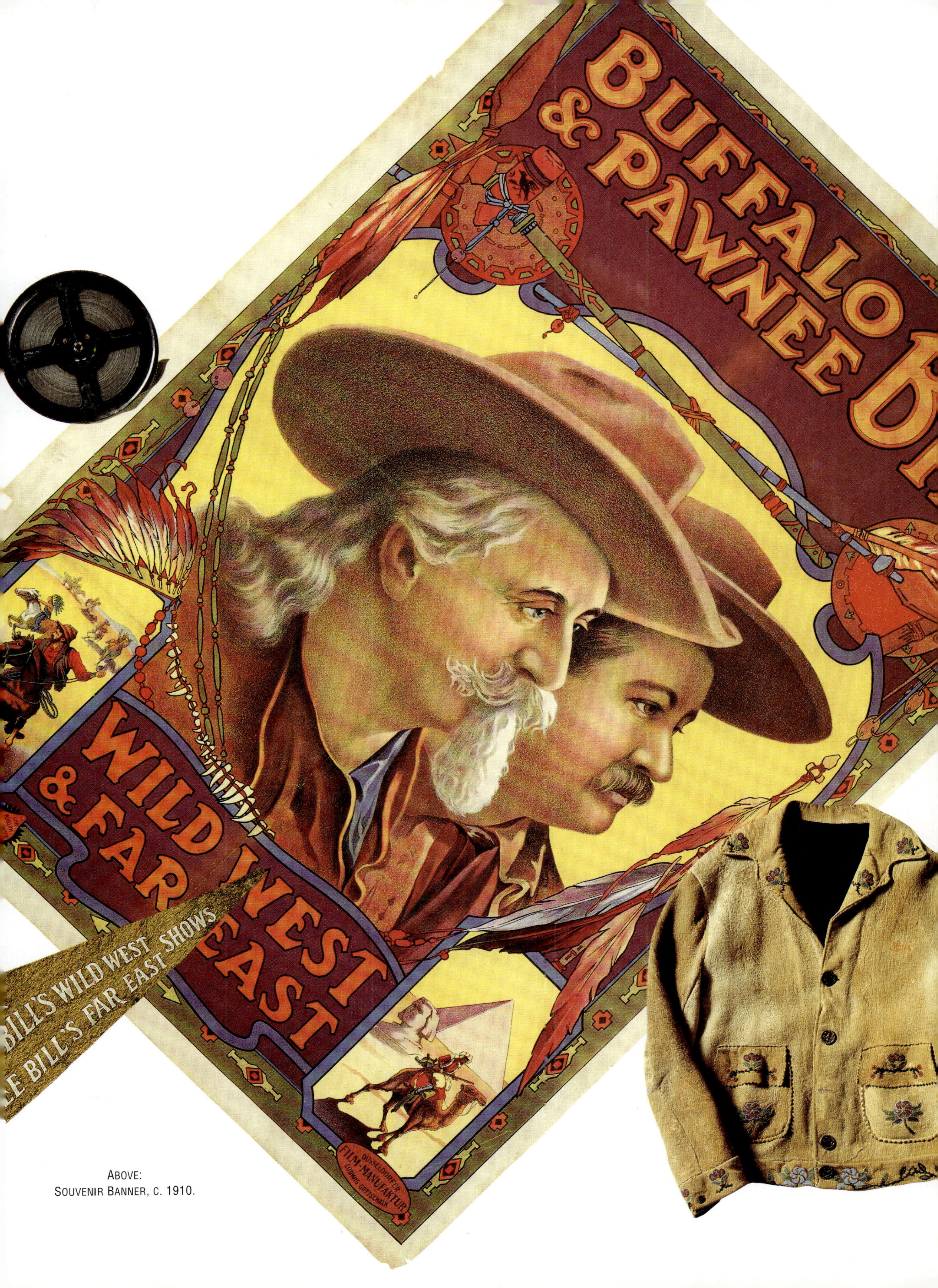

ABOVE:
SOUVENIR BANNER, C. 1910.

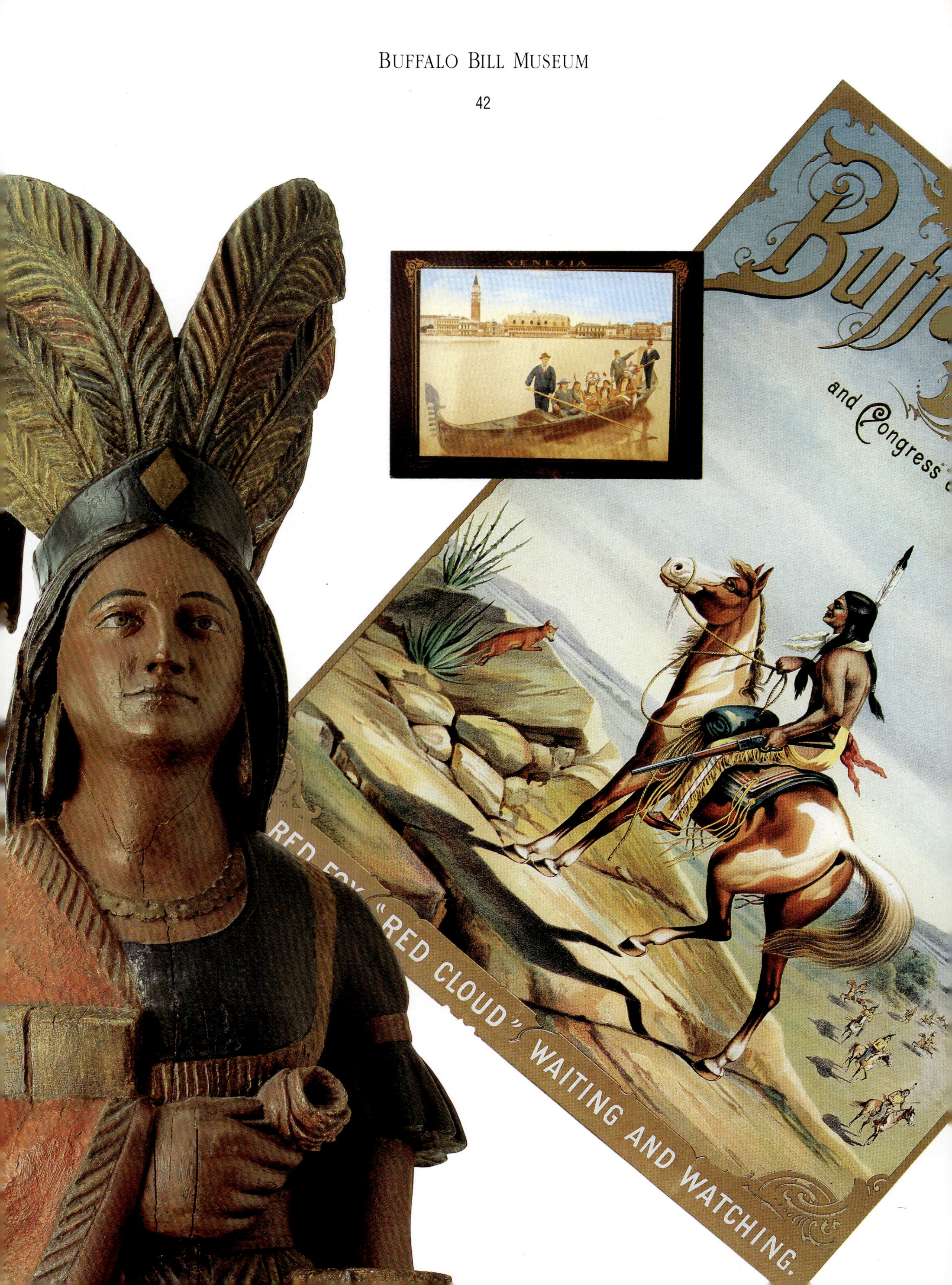
VENEZIA
Buff
and Congress
RED FOX "RED CLOUD" WAITING AND WATCHING.

BELOW:
THE RED FOX, "RED CLOUD," WAITING AND WATCHING, 1893.
A. HOEN & CO., BALTIMORE.
Ambivalence toward American Indians characterized Wild West show productions. In this poster, Red Cloud's association with fox-like cunning and craftiness does not detract from his gallant and confident bearing.

FAR LEFT:
BUFFALO BILL'S WILD WEST IN VENICE, 1890.
ORIGINAL PHOTOGRAPH BY SALVIATI.
Touring the Wild West enabled influential men such as Black Elk and Red Shirt to study white cultures which accepted them and their people with curiosity rather than suspicion. At least two American Indian performers left the show to marry Europeans.

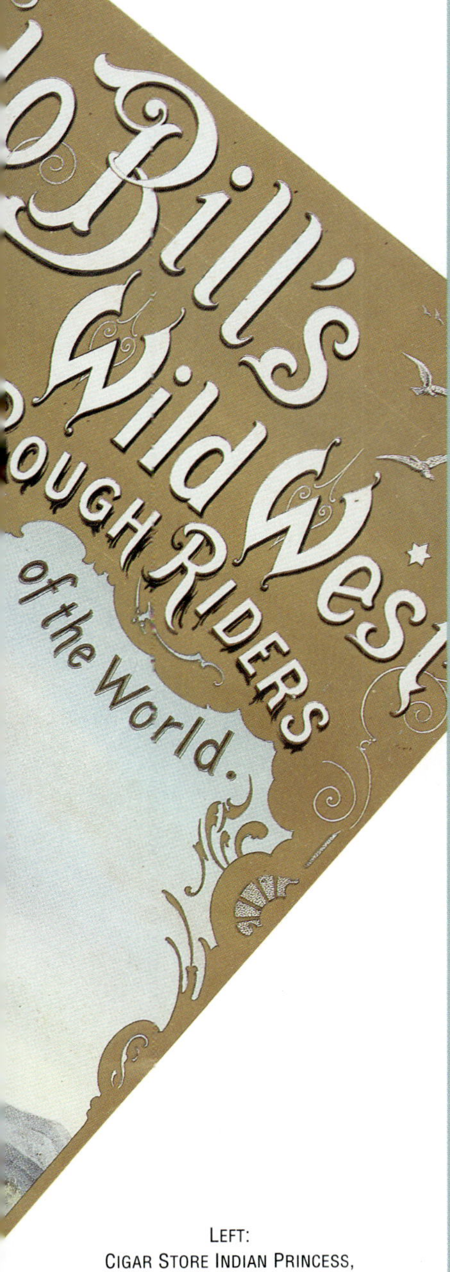

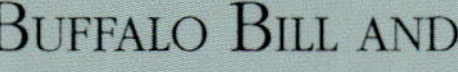

BUFFALO BILL AND THE INDIANS

As early as 1878, Cody was quoted as saying, "Every Indian outbreak that I have ever known has resulted from broken promises and broken treaties by the government." When he was asked for his solution to the Indian "problem," he replied, "never make a single promise to the Indians that is not fulfilled."

Indians of his day considered Cody a good friend, and his relationship with them was characterized by mutual respect. America, Cody stressed, was the Indians' heritage. They had only fought for what was theirs and should expect to be treated with fairness and justice. Most of the Indians who toured with the Wild West were veterans of the wars, and many had known Cody on the Plains.

According to Black Elk, Luther Standing Bear and others, the Indians were treated as equals in the arena and behind the scenes. The federal government controlled the number of Indians, most of whom were Sioux, that was allowed to travel with the Wild West.

So on one hand, the Wild West was a profitable and positive experience for most Indian employees. They were encouraged to keep their language and customs. Those who were married could bring their families along.

But because the show concentrated on the Indian Wars period, and because the show employed mostly Sioux and other Northern Plains people, Buffalo Bill's Wild West helped create and disseminate stereotypes of American Indians as war-bonneted warriors on horseback. Those images are perpetuated even today in film and popular literature.

BELOW:
JULIE NELSON, DAUGHTER OF FRONTIERSMAN JOHN Y. NELSON, C. 1890. ORIGINAL PHOTOGRAPH.

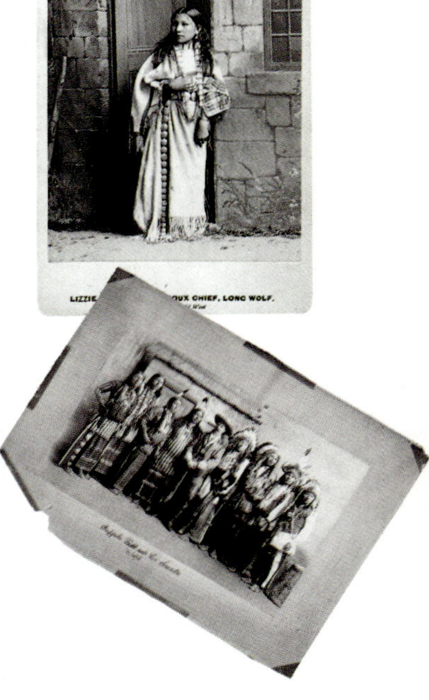

LEFT:
CIGAR STORE INDIAN PRINCESS, C. 1895.
Carved and painted by Samuel Robb, also known for his carousel figures, this statue is representative of the stereotyped association often evoked in 19th-century advertising between American Indians and medicinal plants, including tobacco.

ABOVE:
PAWNEE AND SIOUX PERFORMERS, STATEN ISLAND, C. 1886.
ORIGINAL PHOTOGRAPH BY ANDERSON.
Buffalo Bill (center) is pictured with (from left to right): Brave Chief, Eagle Chief, Knife Chief, Young Chief (Pawnee); American Horse, Rocky Bear, Flies Above, and Long Wolf (Sioux).

Right:
TE Ranch, c. 1900.
Original photograph.
Buffalo Bill established his TE Ranch southwest of Cody in 1895. He adopted the name and registered the brand in Wyoming after acquiring a herd of horses in South Dakota branded "TE."

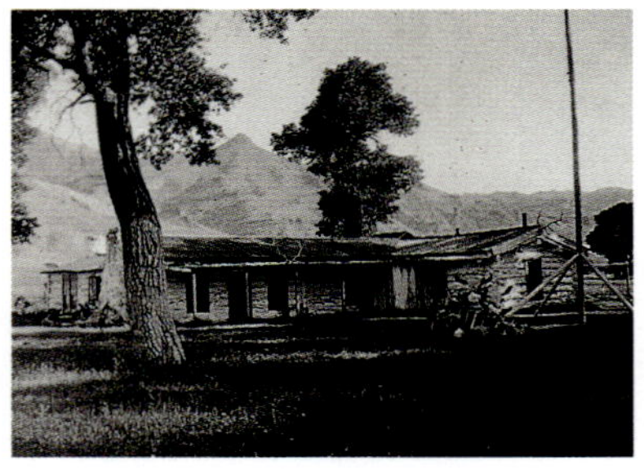

Buffalo Bill's vision of the American frontier was always one of progress and development. His innovations in transportation logistics, employee relations and advertising are, however, sometimes forgotten. He seems representative almost exclusively of the early frontier. Yet, even in Buffalo Bill's lifetime, that frontier outlook was part of a larger belief in settlement and economic growth. In particular, though the ranching way of life symbolizes a past golden age and is currently a source of much nostalgia, Western agricultural development is a story of rapid change and demographic restructuring.

Right:
Plunging Bucker, c. 1895.
Color lithograph.
A. Hoen & Co., Baltimore.
This image of heroic Western daring has been lauded since the era of Buffalo Bill's Wild West. Represented by the cowboy who subdues a beautiful but willful horse, the conquest of nature is a staple Western theme.

Right:
Cowboy's Gear:
Boots, Stetson, rifle and bedroll.
Bedroll is a gift of
Mrs. H. W. Willcutt.
Though Hollywood cowboys are universally laconic, forthright and handsome, real-life cowboys were, in fact, a diverse group who found common ground only in their difficult, underpaid profession. Often their only possessions were their clothes, their rifles and their bedrolls.

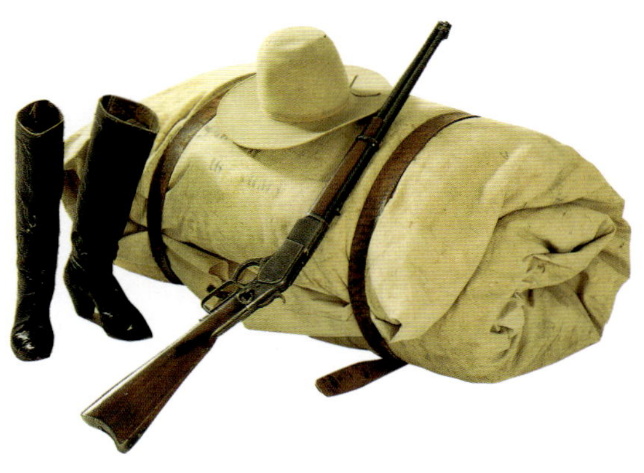

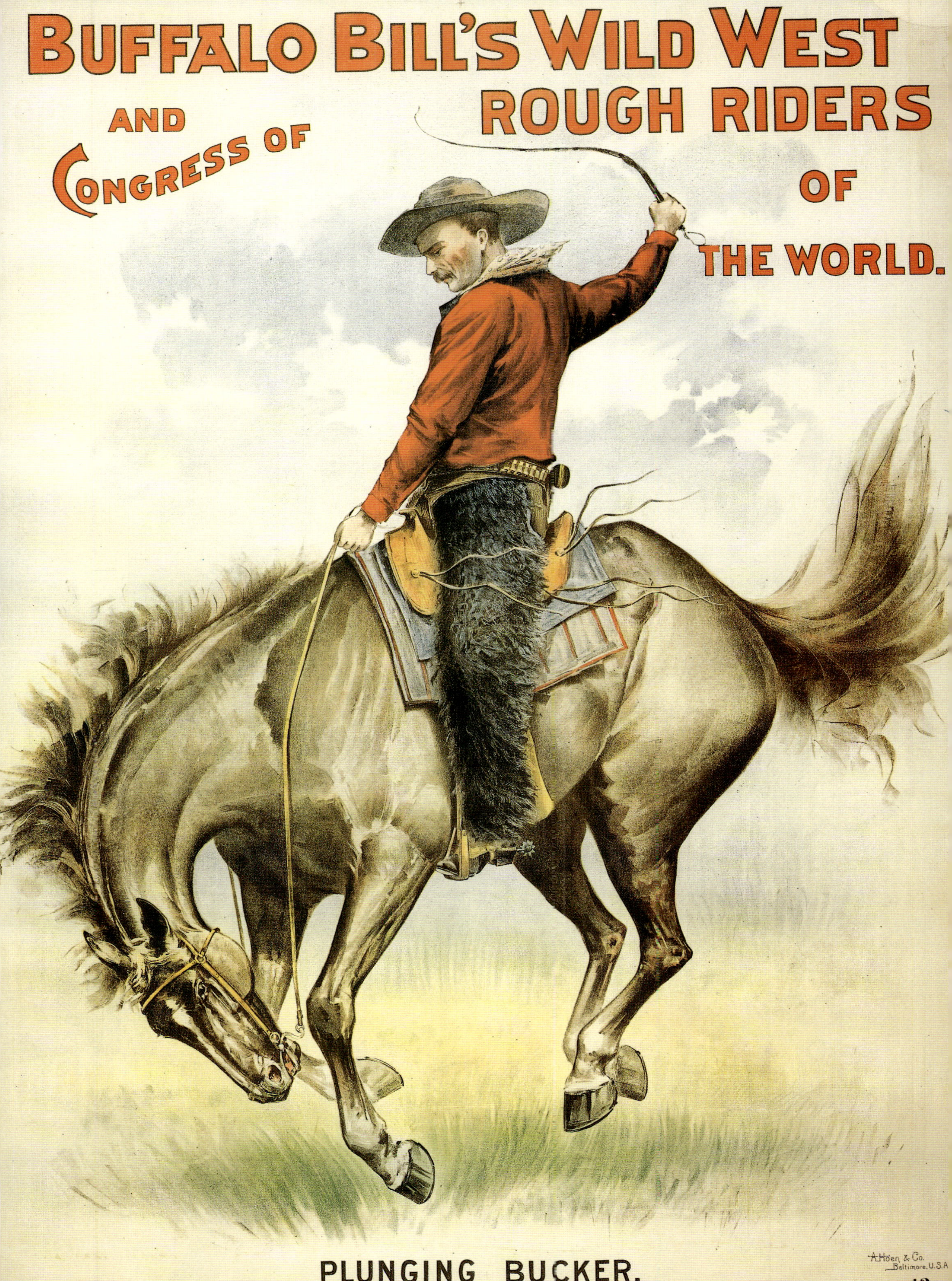
BUFFALO BILL'S WILD WEST
AND
CONGRESS OF
ROUGH RIDERS
OF
THE WORLD.
PLUNGING BUCKER.
A. Hoen & Co.
Baltimore, U.S.A

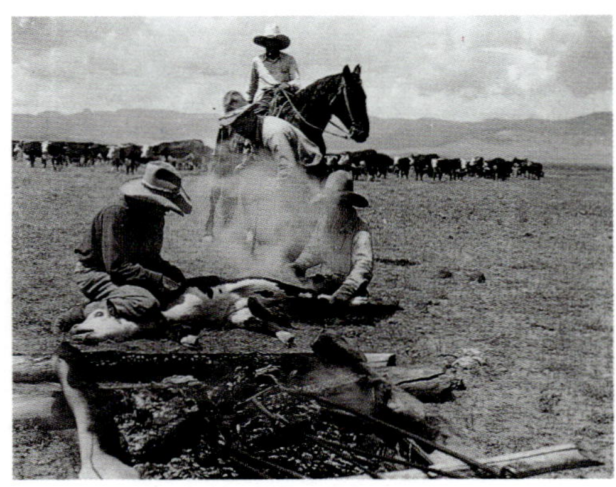

RIGHT:
SPRING BRANDING, C. 1930.
CHARLES BELDEN,
ORIGINAL PHOTOGRAPH.
Calves were branded during spring round-ups. Branding proved ownership when herds mingled on the open range.

Following the Civil War, both Northerners and Southerners saw in the land west of the Mississippi a promise of national unity and personal freedom. Former slaves, youngsters of all races, displaced farmers and former Confederate soldiers headed west to find social equality and economic opportunity. Many of these wanderers eventually came to work as cowhands on large ranches. Considered ruffians and roustabouts at first, they were to enter the national consciousness as folk heroes, inheritors of the reputation for fierce independence formerly bestowed on mountain men and explorers.

The West has never been homogeneous, and the cowboy as a stock character has often been oversimplified. Though Buffalo Bill was instrumental in elevating the cowboy to heroic heights, his and other Wild West shows and early rodeos recognized the cowboy's multi-cultural roots. Almost from the beginning, vaqueros and gauchos were mainstays of the Wild West show. Descendants of a nearly 400-year heritage of ranching and herding in the New World, they gave the cowboy image its costume, equipment and lingo.

Cowboys were also likely to be American Indians or African-Americans. Performer and cowboy Bill Pickett—the inventor of bulldogging as a rodeo event—is perhaps the most famous, but as many as 5,000 black cowboys once rode the range and participated in the great trail drives.

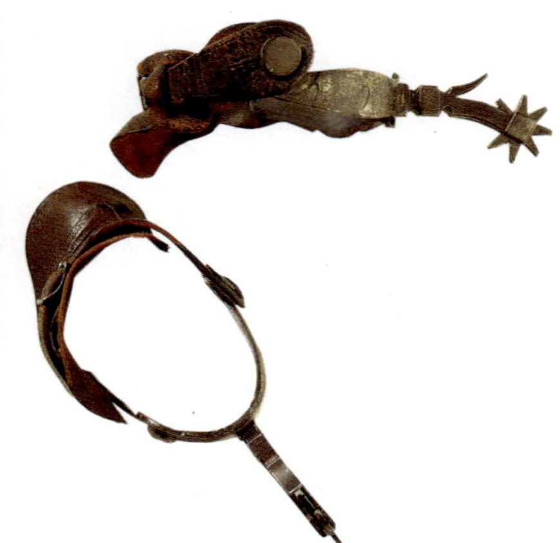

ABOVE:
SPURS, STEEL AND SILVER, 1890.
These spurs belonged to Buffalo Bill and are engraved "Wild West."

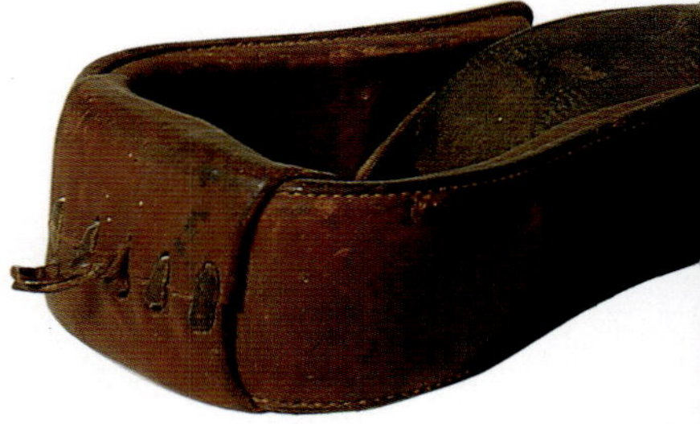

RIGHT:
SADDLE, P.A. WILKERSON,
BUFFALO, WYOMING, C. 1900.
GIFT OF W.H.D. KOERNER III AND
RUTH KOERNER OLIVER.

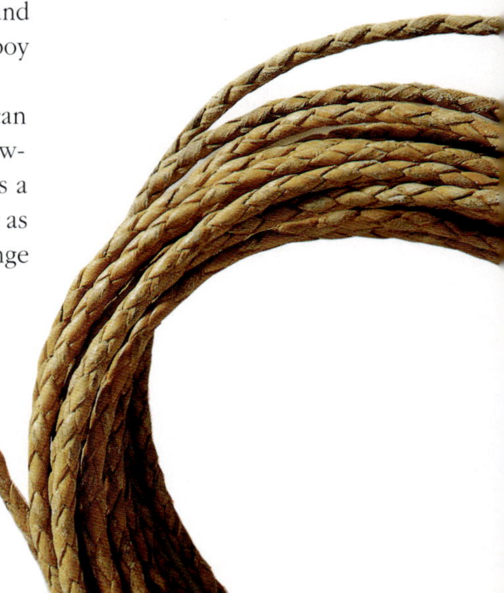

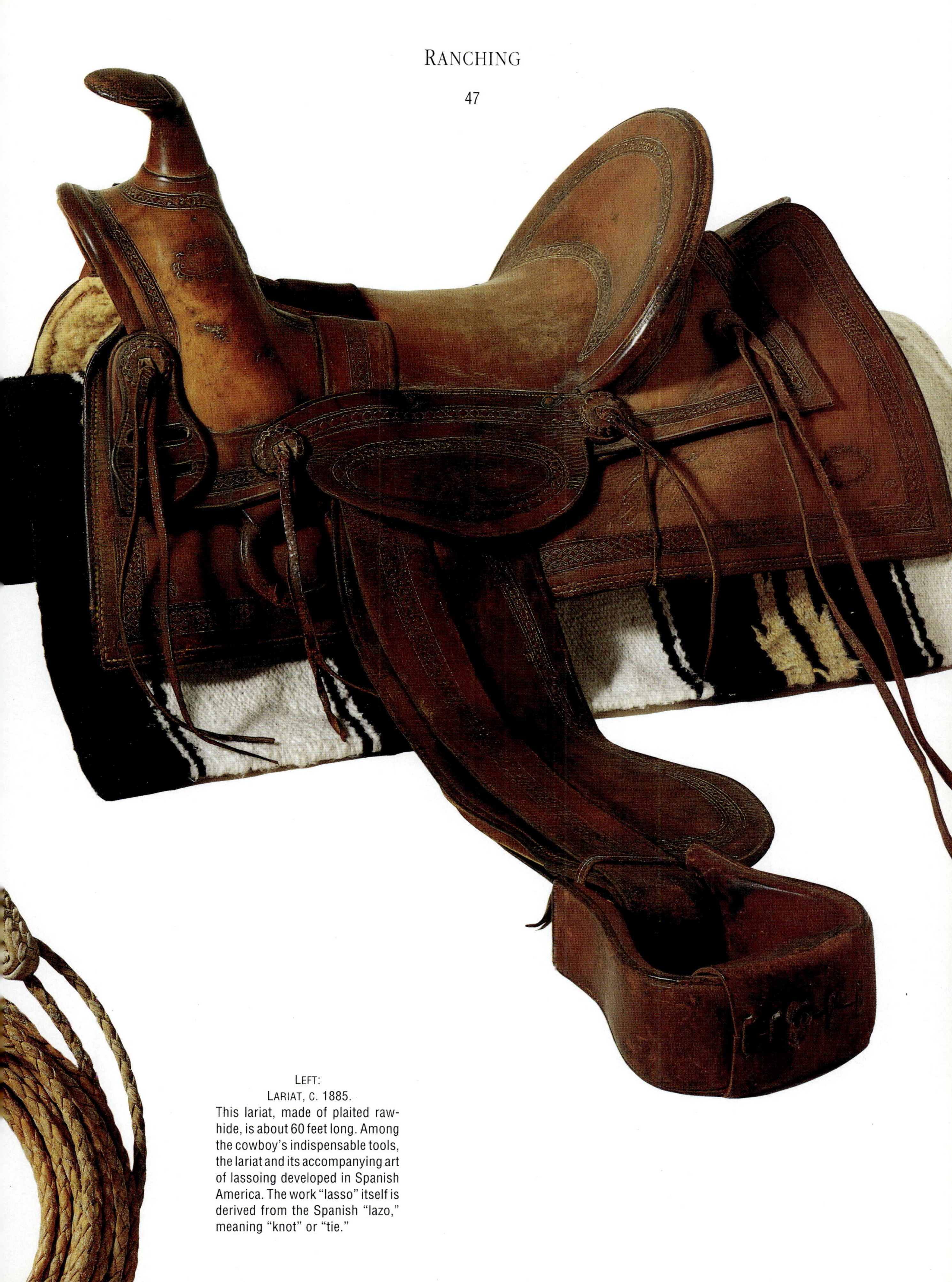

LEFT:
LARIAT, C. 1885.
This lariat, made of plaited rawhide, is about 60 feet long. Among the cowboy's indispensable tools, the lariat and its accompanying art of lassoing developed in Spanish America. The work "lasso" itself is derived from the Spanish "lazo," meaning "knot" or "tie."

BELOW:
MESS WAGON, 1938.
GIFT OF THE H. W. WILLCUTT FAMILY.
Harvey W. Willcutt constructed this wagon for use on his Muddy Creek ranch near Hardin, Montana. According to Willcutt, the wagon's design and equipment were based on years of round-up experience.

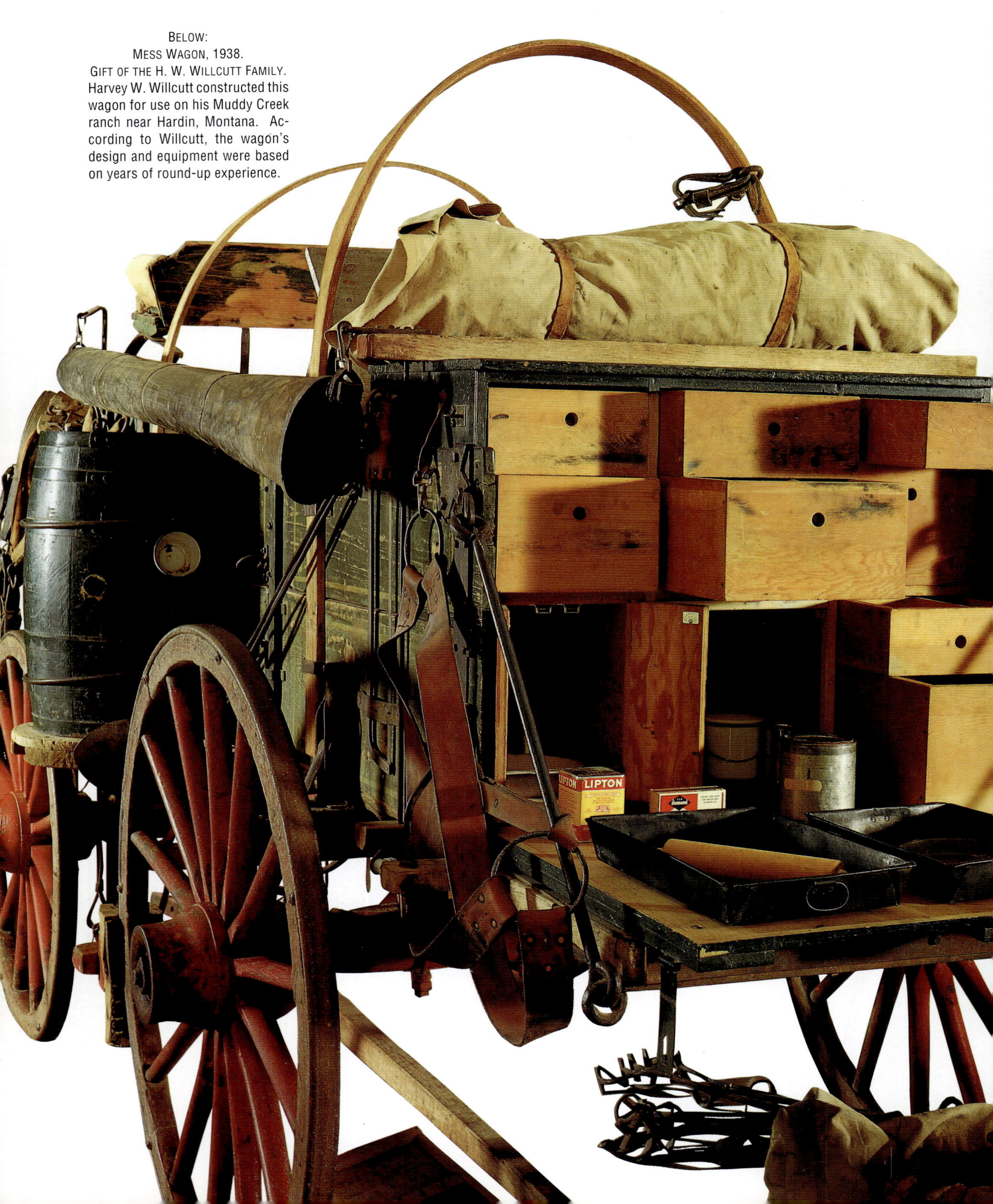

RIGHT:
CHUCK WAGON SING-ALONG, C. 1930. CHARLES BELDEN, ORIGINAL PHOTOGRAPH.
Singing around the campfire is a well-established cowboy tradition. Cowboy songs, both traditional and contemporary, are performed annually at the Buffalo Bill Historical Center's *Cowboy Songs & Range Ballads* program.

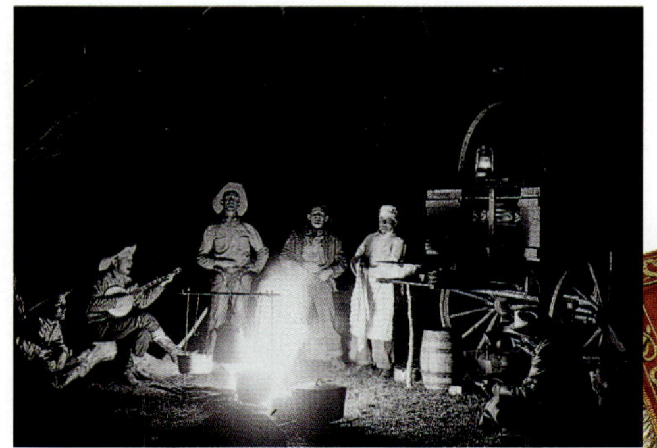

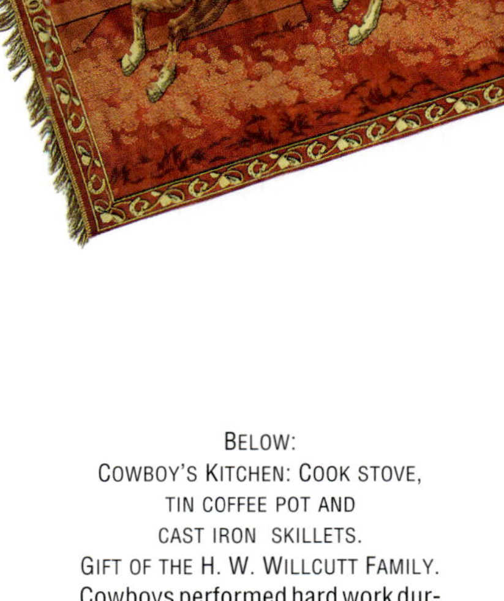

FAR RIGHT:
ITALIAN RUG, C. 1920.
GIFT OF MR. & MRS. CLYDE ERSKINE.
This rug once hung in the office of Montana's OTO Ranch just north of Yellowstone National Park. Founded by J.N. "Dick" Randall and his wife Dora, the OTO was among the first ranches open to paying customers.

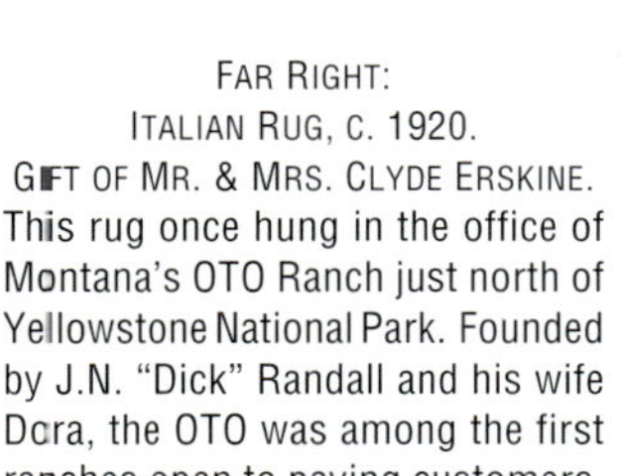

One thing almost all cowboys had in common—and the basis for their popularity as folk heroes—was their independence. Yet they were often underpaid, overworked and subject without recourse to the will of their employers. Especially after ranching spread to the northern Great Plains, owners of large herds exercised enormous power.

With the end of the Indian Wars and the beginning of economic growth heralded by gold strikes in Colorado, Idaho and Montana, the territories of Montana and Wyoming came to be seen as ideal stock raising country. Moreover, railroads enabled ranchers to send their herds directly to midwestern markets. As a result, the industry flourished. Individual ranch-owners joined together to form powerful stockgrower associations. While these organizations often engaged in heavy-handed tactics to keep the open range free of sheep and homesteaders, they improved livestock breeding, supported local artists and artisans, and numbered among their supporters many well-known figures, including Theodore Roosevelt.

Part of the nostalgia that surrounds the era of the open range comes from its brevity. Despite their wealth and power, stockgrowers were soon hit by a string of misfortunes. Overgrazing, flooded markets and an unprecedented series of severe winters put most of the large growers out of business by the late 1880s. Their era persists, though, in the many popular Western traditions to which it gave rise.

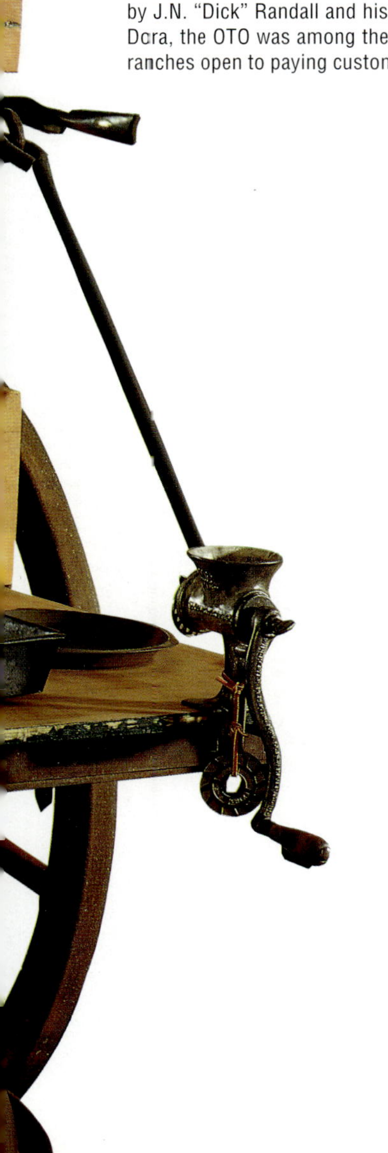

BELOW:
COWBOY'S KITCHEN: COOK STOVE, TIN COFFEE POT AND CAST IRON SKILLETS.
GIFT OF THE H. W. WILLCUTT FAMILY.
Cowboys performed hard work during long hours. Often after the day was over, their only remuneration was a hot meal. Standard fare for cowboys was dark coffee steeped in its own grounds, pinto beans and baking powder biscuits.

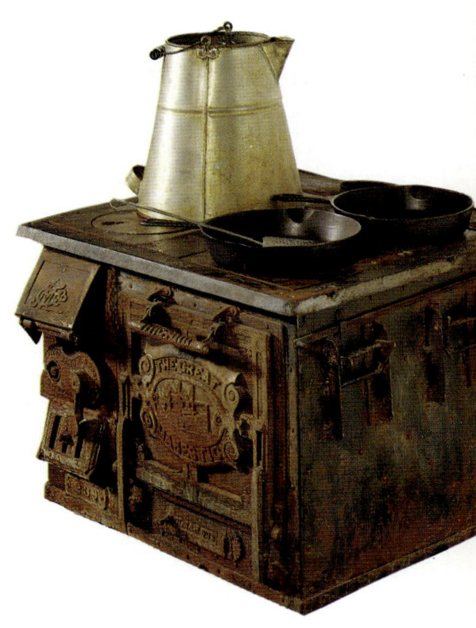

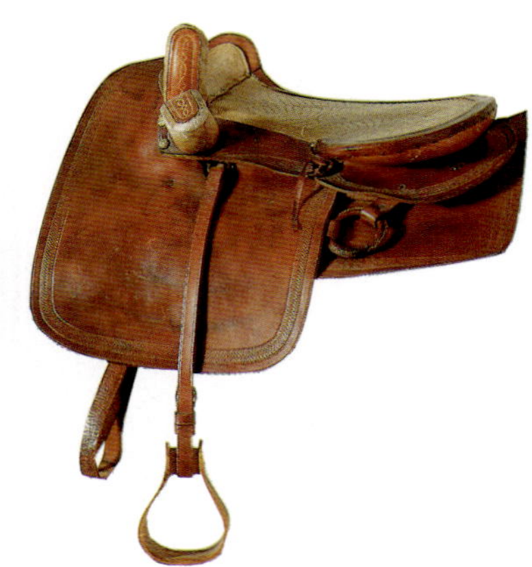

LEFT:
SIDE SADDLE, C. 1890.
This saddle was owned and used by Irma Cody Garlow, Buffalo Bill's daughter, who lived in Cody, Wyoming, and, with her husband, managed the Irma Hotel until their deaths in the influenza epidemic of October 1918.

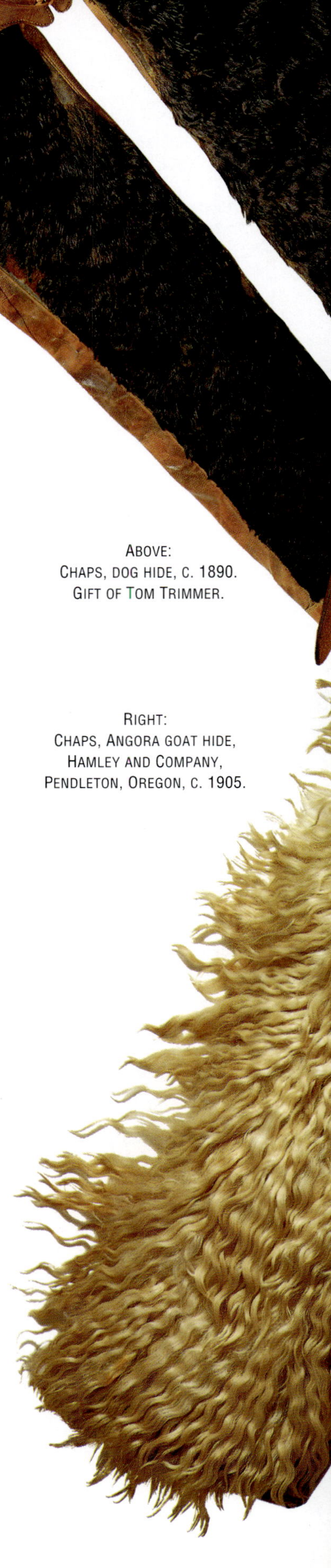

ABOVE:
CHAPS, DOG HIDE, C. 1890.
GIFT OF TOM TRIMMER.

RIGHT:
CHAPS, ANGORA GOAT HIDE,
HAMLEY AND COMPANY,
PENDLETON, OREGON, C. 1905.

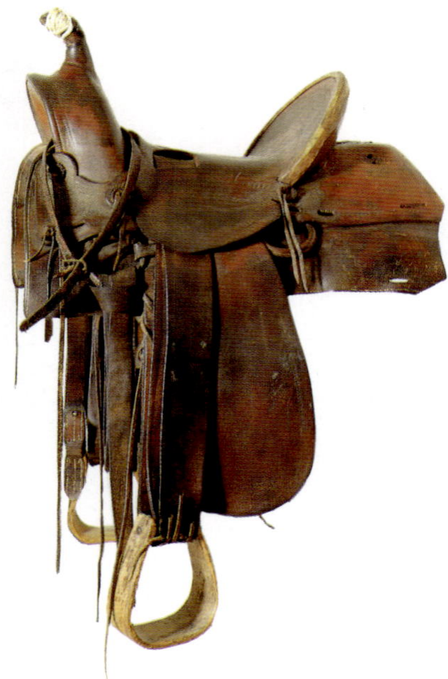

ABOVE:
SADDLE, F.A. MEANA, CHEYENNE, C. 1890.
GIFT OF ROY HOLM.

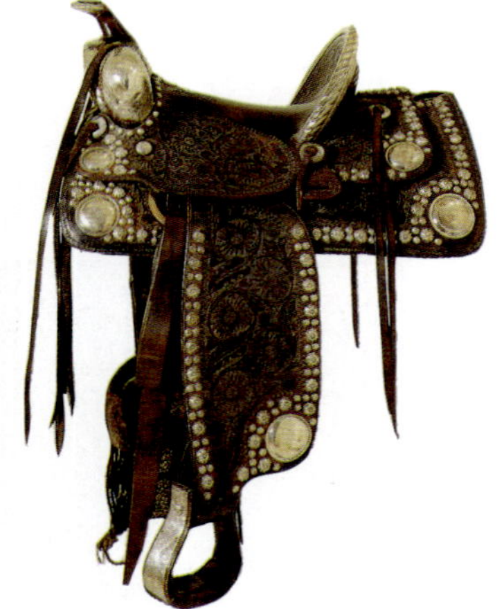

ABOVE:
OTO RANCH SADDLE,
LICHTENBERGER-FERGUSON,
LOS ANGELES, 1925.

Typical Western dress is definitely cowboy. As described by Roosevelt, the cowboys' outfits consisted of "jingling spurs, the big revolvers stuck in their belts and bright silk handkerchiefs knotted loosely round their necks over the open collars of the flannel shirts." Even urban Westerners often emulate this look or some modified version of it.

The cowboy ethic has even more adherents. Irreverence, individuality, an unwillingness to back down from a fair fight, chivalrous treatment of women and children have become national values. Even U.S. global politics is often modeled on the cowboy's example—genteel, but cool, he defends the weak and faces the enemy with just the right measure of arrogance.

Western hospitality and camaraderie were also born during the ranching era. Though cowboys were a diverse group, most preferred the solitary life of riding the property line checking for strays, moving the herds to fresh grassland and water, treating animal diseases, breaking horses, or, in later years, checking fences for breaks or damage. Yet some occasions brought them joyously together.

In spring and fall groups of ranchers brought all cattle in the area to a central location, then separated them back into their proper herds. Branding, de-horning, and castrating took place in the spring, and in fall the cattle to be sold were cut out of the herd.

Such round-ups could last four weeks or longer, and though they involved hard work, they were also important social events. Neighbors, friends and cowboys from remote ranches got together to share news, eat good food and show off their roping and riding. Cowboys arranged competitions that later evolved into modern-day rodeo events.

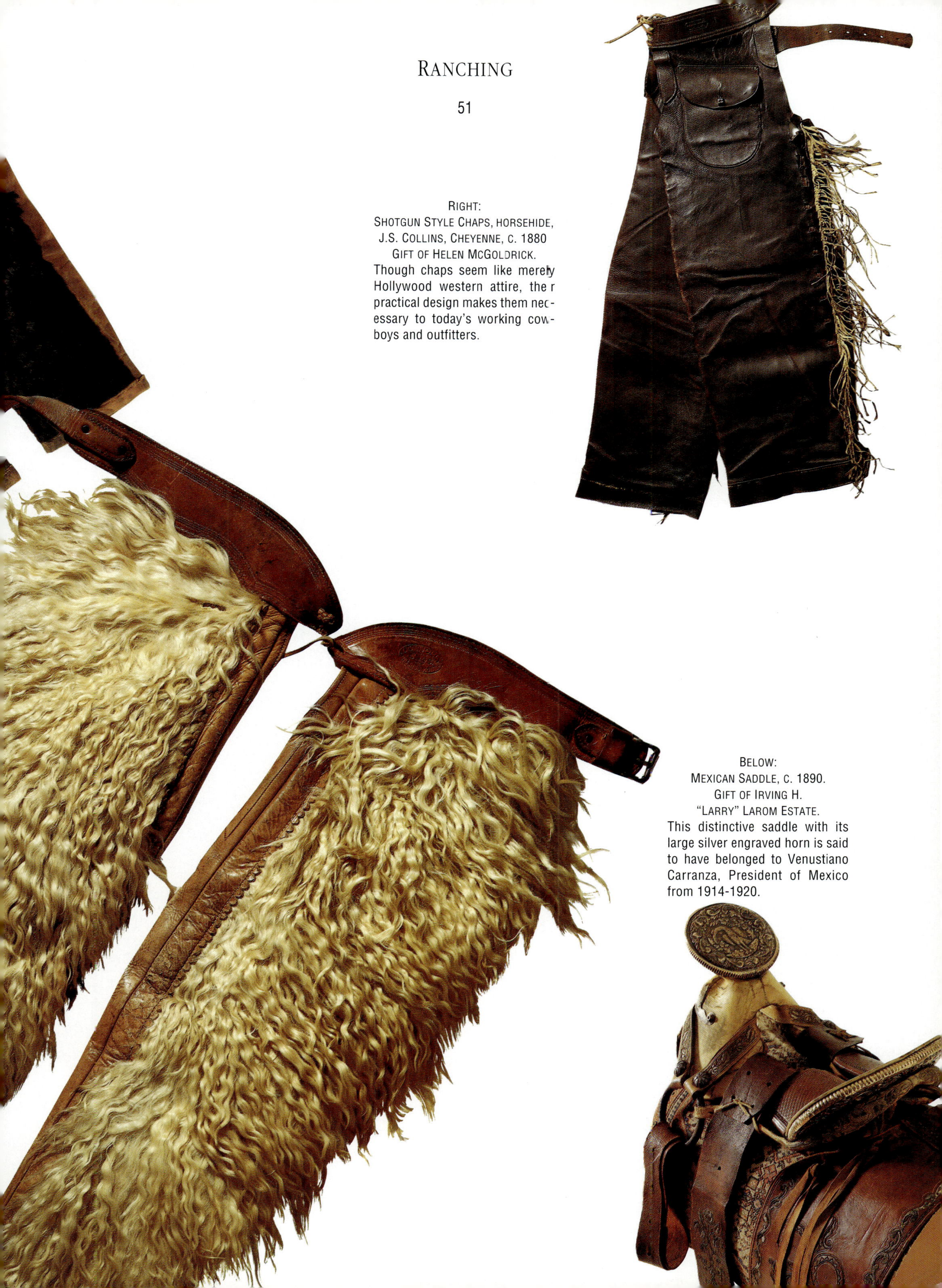

RIGHT:
SHOTGUN STYLE CHAPS, HORSEHIDE, J.S. COLLINS, CHEYENNE, C. 1880
GIFT OF HELEN MCGOLDRICK.
Though chaps seem like merely Hollywood western attire, their practical design makes them necessary to today's working cowboys and outfitters.

BELOW:
MEXICAN SADDLE, C. 1890.
GIFT OF IRVING H. "LARRY" LAROM ESTATE.
This distinctive saddle with its large silver engraved horn is said to have belonged to Venustiano Carranza, President of Mexico from 1914-1920.

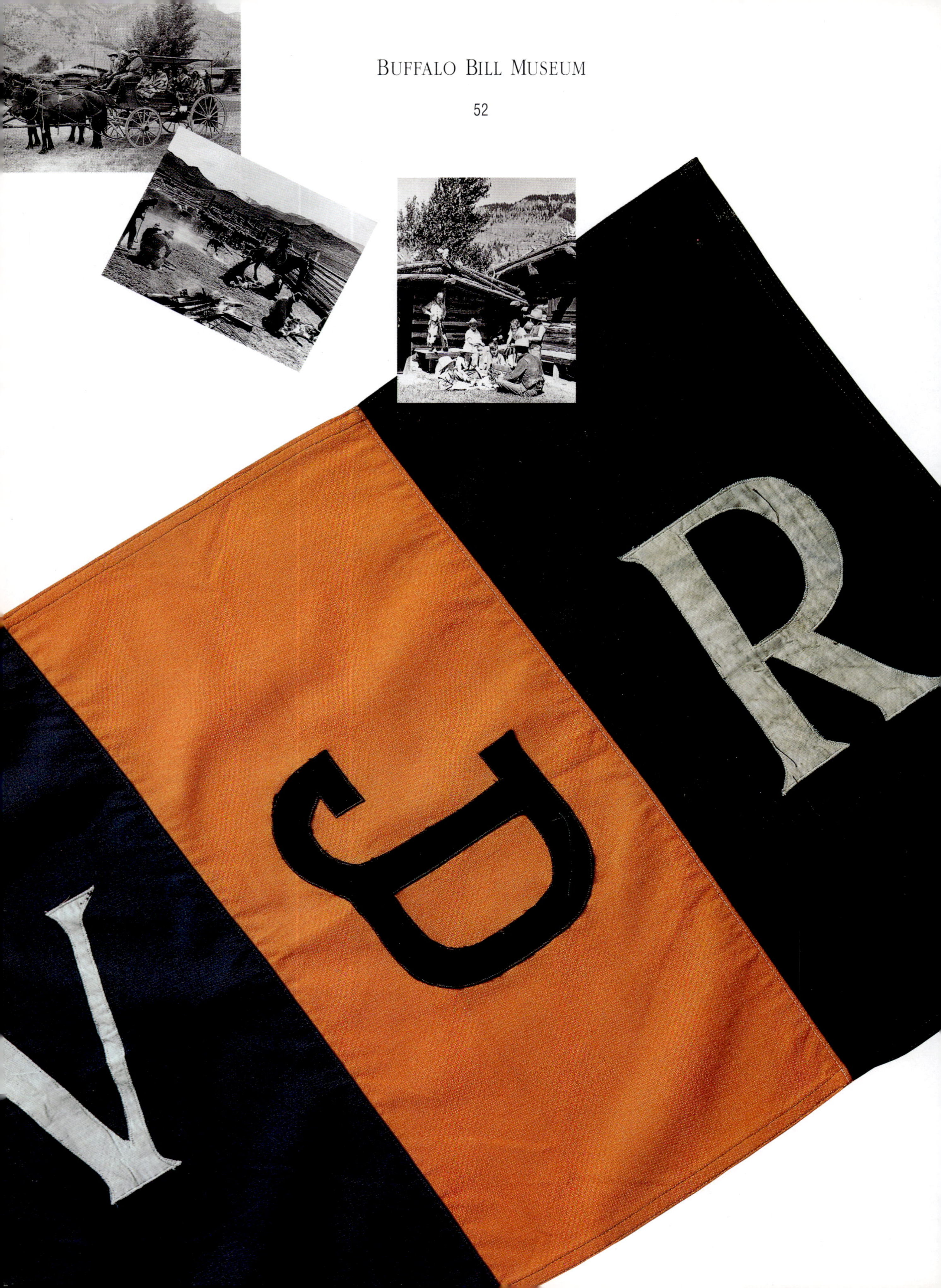

LEFT:
DUDES IN CODY COUNTRY NEAR YELLOWSTONE NATIONAL PARK,
1910 - 1930.
ORIGINAL PHOTOGRAPHS.

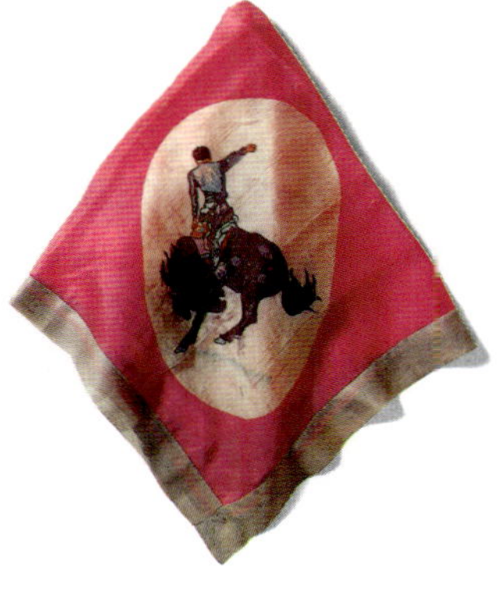

LEFT:
SOUVENIR SCARF,
MILES CITY ROUNDUP, 1916.
GIFT OF MRS. LEOLA ZELLER IN MEMORY OF ELVA FREDERICKSON.
Competitive rodeo became popular at the same time as Wild West shows began to decline. Ranch skills such as bronc busting and steer roping are now well-known arena events.

LEFT:
FLAG, VALLEY RANCH, C. 1930.
GIFT OF IRVING H. "LARRY" LAROM ESTATE.
The Valley Ranch was originally homesteaded by "Sunny Jim" and "Buckskin Jenny" McLaughlin. New York City native Larry Larom purchased it from them in 1915.

Another staple Western phenomenon was born during the late 1800s. What is credited as the first operating dude ranch was founded by brothers Howard, Alden and Willis Eaton in Medora, North Dakota. Realizing that city folk (or dudes) who wanted to sample Western life might be a source of substantial income, they began charging such visitors for the privilege of staying at a working ranch. The OTO, owned by J.N. "Dick" Randall and Dora Roseborough Randall, included a post office at "Dude Ranch, Montana" and became a leader in wildlife conservation. Similarly, the Valley Ranch owned by Irma and I.H. "Larry" Larom became an active partner in local development and conservation.

Recognizing the economic potential of tourism, dude ranchers joined with the railroads to promote Western travel. Rather than simply extracting wealth from the land, they saw possibilities in conserving it. Today, dude ranching remains an important part of Western culture, preserving and perpetuating the region's history, maintaining the heritage of the cowboy, providing regional economic stability and promoting conservation of the West's wildlife resources.

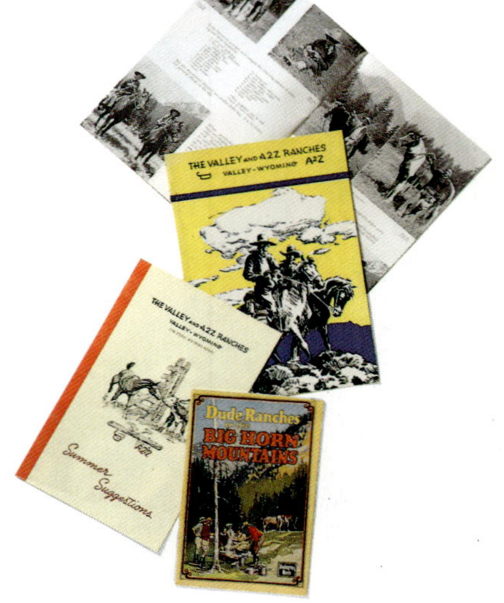

ABOVE:
DUDE RANCH BROCHURES.
Railroads which carried tourists west often formed advertising alliances with dude ranchers.

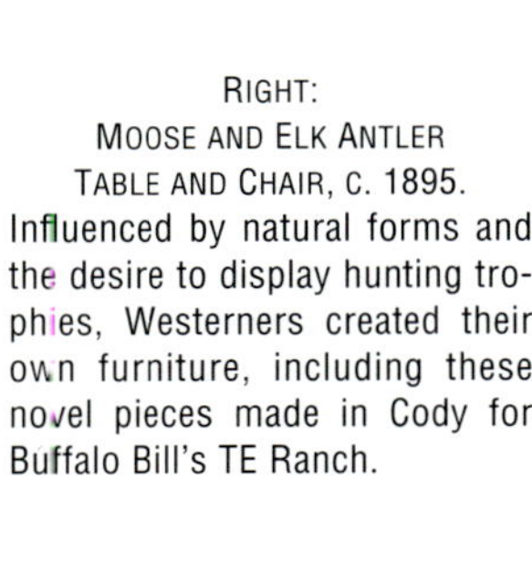

RIGHT:
MOOSE AND ELK ANTLER TABLE AND CHAIR, C. 1895.
Influenced by natural forms and the desire to display hunting trophies, Westerners created their own furniture, including these novel pieces made in Cody for Buffalo Bill's TE Ranch.

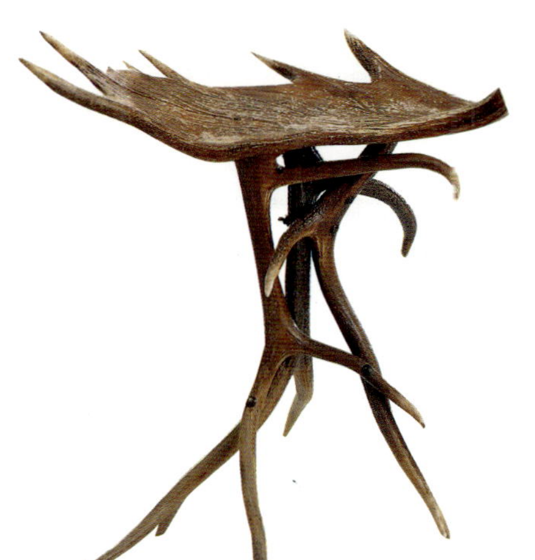

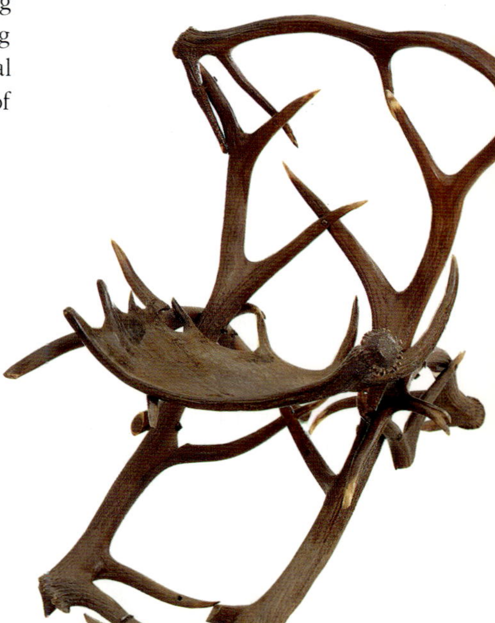

BUFFALO BILL MUSEUM

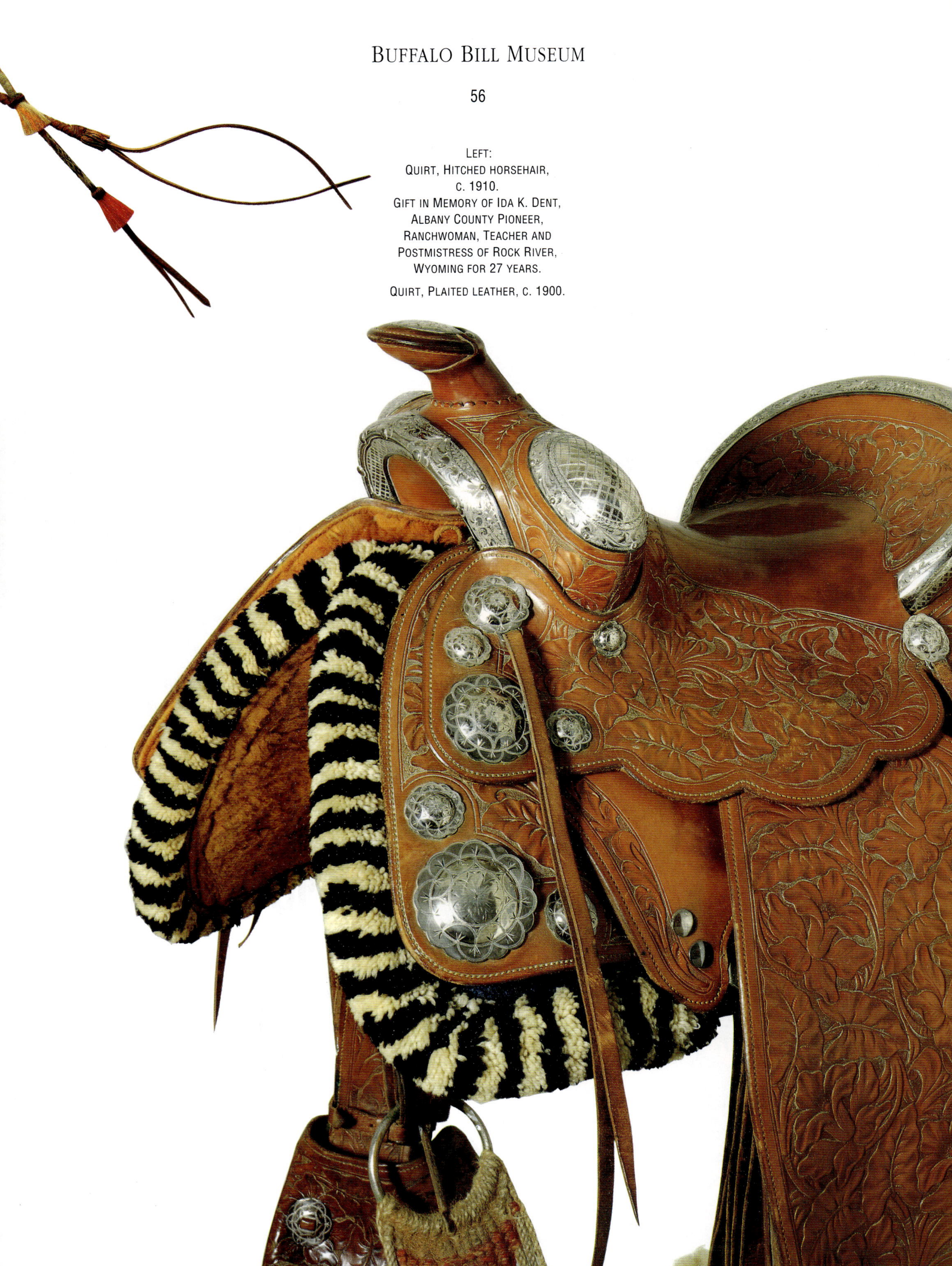

LEFT:
QUIRT, HITCHED HORSEHAIR,
C. 1910.
GIFT IN MEMORY OF IDA K. DENT,
ALBANY COUNTY PIONEER,
RANCHWOMAN, TEACHER AND
POSTMISTRESS OF ROCK RIVER,
WYOMING FOR 27 YEARS.

QUIRT, PLAITED LEATHER, C. 1900.

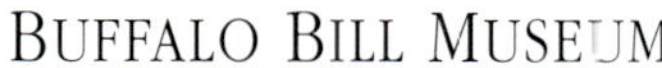

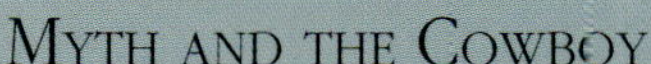

MYTH AND THE COWBOY

A myth is a story that helps explain our world. The story might be imaginary, or it may be mostly true. The important thing is that it helps us to understand what kind of people we are.

For example, the life stories of George Washington and Abraham Lincoln are important American myths. They provide images to live up to. They define ideal American political leaders.

Stories about taming the West are part of American myth, and the cowboy is a mythic character in America. We admire him for his independence, his honesty, his modesty and courage. He represents the best in all Americans as he stares down evil and says, "When you call me that, smile."

In fact, these traits were necessary to survival, along with a code of behavior which included loyalty and cooperation. Herding cattle on the vast plains was a lonely, low-paying and dangerous job. Cowboys had varied backgrounds. Many were blacks who found it difficult to get other jobs. Their diversity made them appear colorful and romantic to newspaper writers.

Not all the mythic attributes of the cowboy are considered admirable. The United States has often been accused, for example, of practicing "cowboy diplomacy," shooting first (out of ignorance) and asking questions later.

In fact, before the 1880s, cowboys were also considered to be hooligans and ruffians. Buffalo Bill's Wild West, along with the illustrations of Frederic Remington and other artists, helped make them popular heroes. The first "King of the Cowboys" was Buck Taylor, a 6-foot 6-inch Texan in Buffalo Bill's Wild West. He was a soft-spoken gentleman, but he could also ride, rope, shoot and rescue damsels in distress.

ABOVE LEFT:
SADDLER'S TOOLS
(FROM LEFT TO RIGHT):
MALLET, ROUND KNIFE, EDGER AND ROSETTE PUNCH.
GIFT OF VICTOR ALEXANDER, JR.
From the collection of famed saddlemaker Victor Alexander, these tools represent just some of the equipment needed to stretch, mold, sew, stamp, cut and emboss saddle leather.

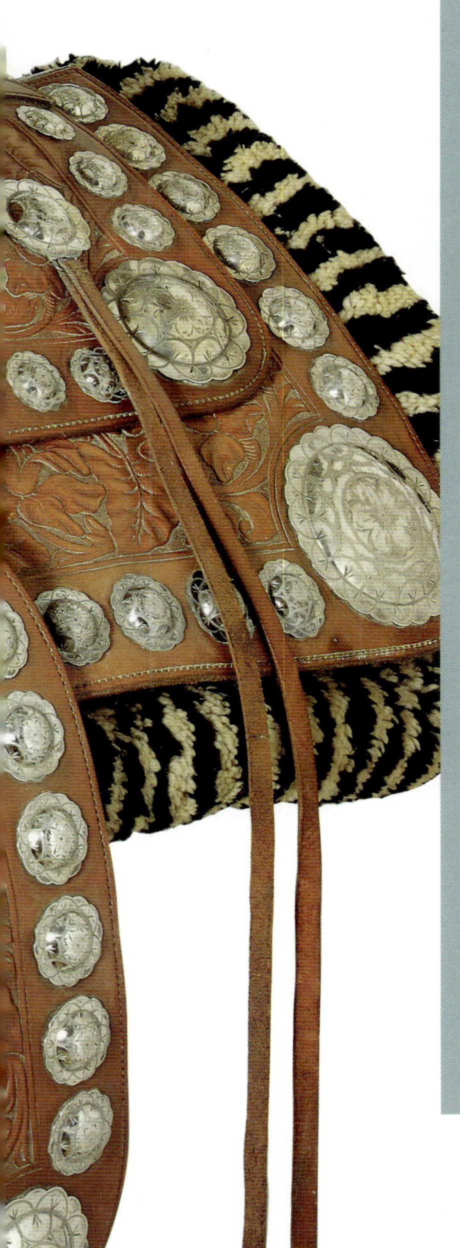

LEFT:
SADDLE,
VICTOR ALEXANDER COMPANY,
HAYWARD, CALIFORNIA, C. 1942
GIFT OF MARK MAYER.
As a young man, Victor Alexander (1906-1973) worked on dude ranches near Cody and in rodeos. In the 1930s he became a saddlemaker in California, where he founded the Victor Alexander Company. For more than 20 years, he was chief of design and production for the Bona Allen Saddle Company of Buford, Georgia, whose products were widely sold through Sears, Roebuck and other catalogues.

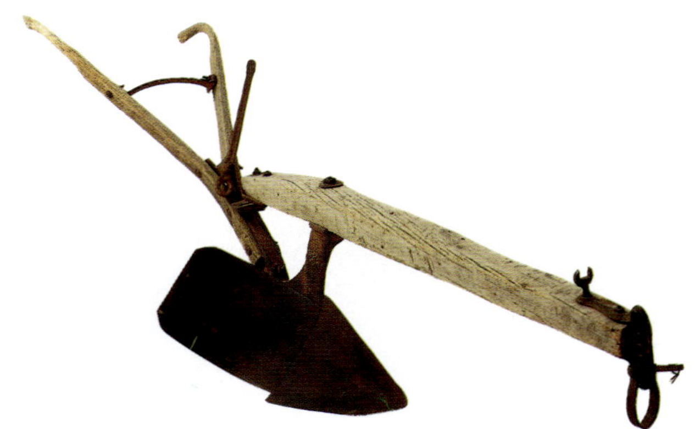

RIGHT:
PLOUGH, WOOD AND CAST IRON, C. 1890.
GIFT OF DAVE WASDEN.
Of thousands who traveled the Oregon Trail, few could envision the high prairies and mountain valleys as suitable agricultural land. Only when irrigation was available did these regions attract farmers. Mormon pioneers established the first farms in the Big Horn Basin.

Because of its arid geography, the West has always had a higher proportion of town dwellers than other regions. Settlement required centralized commerce, transportation and irrigation. At first, towns arose at the sites of military forts and trading posts. Later, communities achieved permanence by serving local farming and ranching populations. A few were established by religious sects desiring their own commercial and social centers. The common thread in Western development, though, is difficulty.

RIGHT:
SHOSHONE IRRIGATION COMPANY ADVERTISEMENT, 1899.
Kentuckian George Beck, Banker Horace Alger, Engineer C. E. Hayden, Nate Salsbury, and Buffalo Bill were among the founders of the Shoshone Irrigation Company, the aim of which was to build a dam and a canal in the Big Horn Basin and open its desert lands to agriculture.

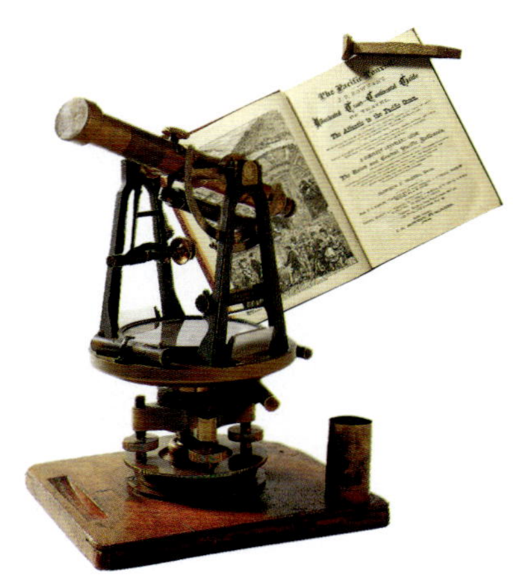

RIGHT:
TOOLS OF EMPIRE: SURVEYOR'S TRANSIT AND BOX, C. 1890.
MANUFACTURED BY BUFF AND BERGER. COURTESY OF PARK COUNTY HISTORICAL SOCIETY.

GOLDEN SPIKE REPLICA.
In 1895, Charles E. Hayden surveyed a Cody canal route and townsite for the Shoshone Irrigation Company. By 1901, the arrival of the railroad provided an essential link to eastern trading centers.

Shoshone Irrigation Company,

OWNERS OF THE CODY CANAL.

Has Water Ready for Thousands of Acres of Good State Lands.

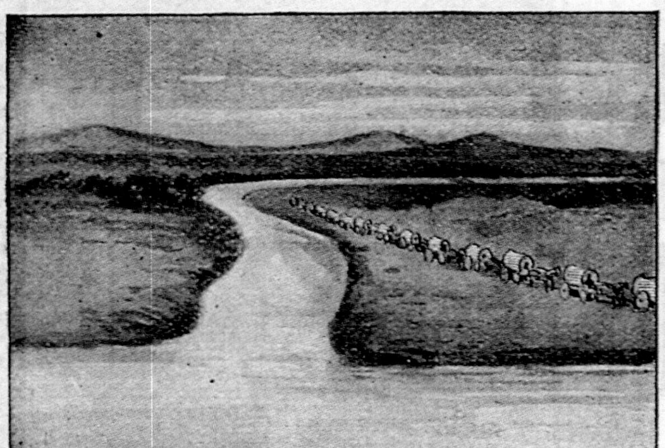

UNLIMITED WATER WAITS THE CULTIVATOR, FINE LAND WAITS THE PLOW.

LETTER FROM STATE ENGINEER.

STATE OF WYOMING,
ELWOOD MEAD, STATE ENGINEER,
CHEYENNE, WYO., DEC. 22, 1896.

SHOSHONE IRRIGATION CO., CODY, WYOMING:

GENTLEMEN.—I regard the Cody Canal as one of the most important and valuable projects ever inaugurated in this State, and believe it is destined to exercise great influence on our growth in wealth and population.

It will open to settlers a region having vast and varied resources. I know of no place in this country which offers to prudent and industrious farmers greater assurances of material prosperity and physical comfort than the Big Horn Basin.

This valley has a local climate, with less snow-fall in the winter than any part of the surrounding country, and with a mean temperature in summer which permits of a wider diversity of crops than is possible in much of the country five hundred miles south of it. It is, therefore, equally well adapted to the purposes of the stock raiser, grain grower, fruit raiser, or market gardener.

The Cody Canal takes its water supply from one of the largest rivers in the West, and reclaims some of the best land in this State. The completed portion is well and substantially built with an ample capacity to water all the land below it.

The price of shares therein is as low as the cost of the work will permit; the conditions of purchase absolutely fair to water users.

The ultimate ownership of both Canal and land by settlers, with the abundant water supply, gives the cultivators of these lands a security and independence not always enjoyed by irrigators.

I can, therefore, unreservedly and heartily commend your project to investors and the lands it waters to homeseekers.

Respectfully, ELWOOD MEAD, State Engineer.

TITLES TO HOMES PERFECT.

TITLES TO THE LAND FROM THE UNITED STATES TO THE STATE OF WYOMING.

FROM THE STATE OF WYOMING FOR BOTH LAND AND WATER TO THE PURCHASER.

Comparative Cost of Land.—The price of irrigated land varies in the different localities. Taking the arid region as a whole, the average price varies from $50 to $100 per acre. In California it ranges from $50 to $400; in Arizona from $25 to $100; in Washington from $55 to $100, and in Western Colorado from $50 to $100. In all States there are lands suited only to the cultivation of grasses and cereals which may be had from $25 upwards. But for lands under the Cody Canal which can produce such a variety of crops the price asked is remarkably low, for it must be remembered that you secure not only the land but a perpetual water right.

The State charges only 50 cents per acre for the land (and $2 fee for completing title), but requires of the settler that he shall show evidence of contract with the Irrigation Company for the water right requisite to make his land of any use, and the Company's price is $10 per acre. This need not all be paid at once, however. It can be paid in five annual installments, with simply the addition of 6 per cent. interest.

PRICES REASONABLE AND IN SMALL PAYMENTS.

COL. W. F. CODY, President.

Full information can be obtained concerning procurements of this land by prospective settlers from

GEO. T. BECK, Manager and Secretary,

BIG HORN COUNTY. CODY, WYOMING.

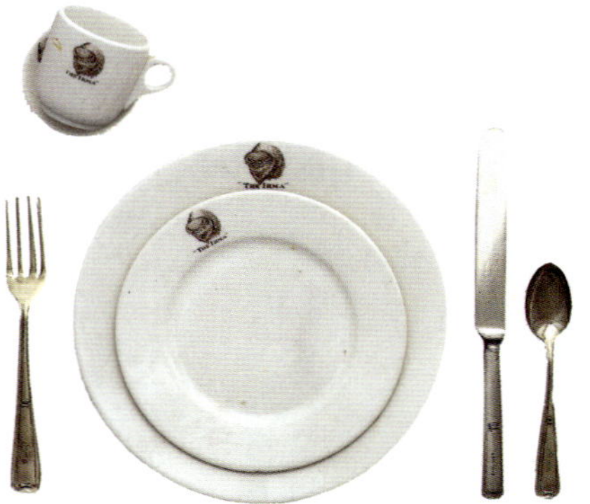

RIGHT:
HOSE CART, C. 1905.
COURTESY OF
CODY VOLUNTEER FIRE DEPARTMENT.
Once they had built enough that was worth saving, Cody's developers manned and equipped the Cody Volunteer Fire Department. In general, volunteer associations were an important component of emerging towns.

ABOVE RIGHT:
FLATWARE AND SILVERWARE
FROM THE IRMA, C. 1902.
Buffalo Bill's hotel in Cody, completed in 1902, opened with much fanfare. Visiting reporter Charles Wayland Towne noted that "a thousand guests gaped at the rich draperies, polished floors, (and) shiny oak furniture . . . bathed in the light of chandeliers fed by acetylene gas."

BELOW:
ADVERTISING SHINGLE AND
MEDICAL BAG, C. 1910.
GIFT OF MARGERY GIBSON ROSS.
House physician for The Irma, Dr. Frances Lane also cared for workers hired on for the Shoshone Dam project between 1905 and 1910. Like many other Western women who studied medicine, Dr. Lane offered specialized skills a small frontier town could ill afford to refuse.

To flourish, townspeople had to work together and endure formidable isolation, harsh weather and economic uncertainty. Successful towns needed to be, above all else, intradependent communities.

But making the transition from frontier outpost to genuine town required more than the dedication of a town's citizenry. A newspaper was one of the foremost necessities. Its function was to draw potential immigrants by using what Cody pioneer Charles Hayden called "big, very interesting and glowing adjectives" to describe a settlement and its surroundings.

Tradesmen such as saddlers and blacksmiths were also necessary. Skilled craftsmen performed a variety of tasks in rendering a settlement relatively self-sufficient and prosperous. Saddlemakers, for example, often worked with leather goods of all kinds, including reins, bridles, horse collars, pistol holsters and occasionally even boots and shoes.

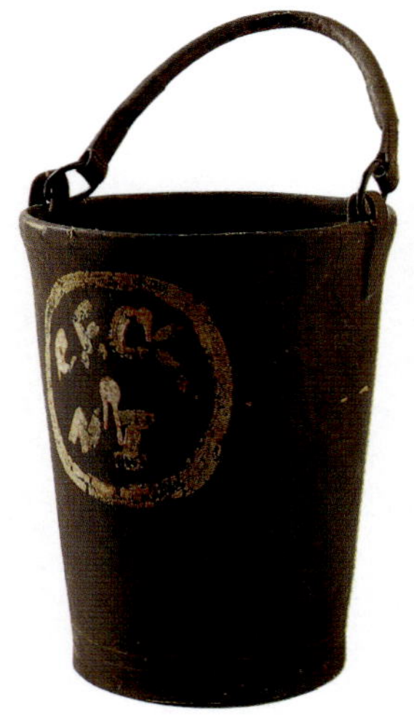

ABOVE:
WATER BUCKET, CANVAS
AND RUBBER, C. 1905.
COURTESY OF
STANLEY N. LANDGREN.
The devastation fire could wreak on a small town was magnified by Western distance. New building materials such as nails and even lumber might be several days' journey away. This bucket, like the hose cart at right, was used by the Cody Volunteer Fire Department.

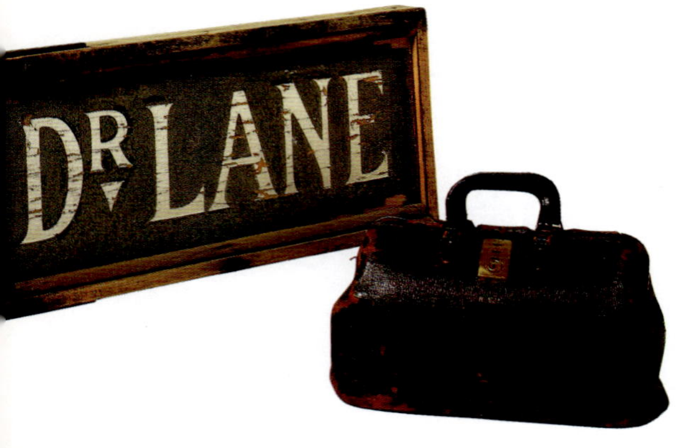

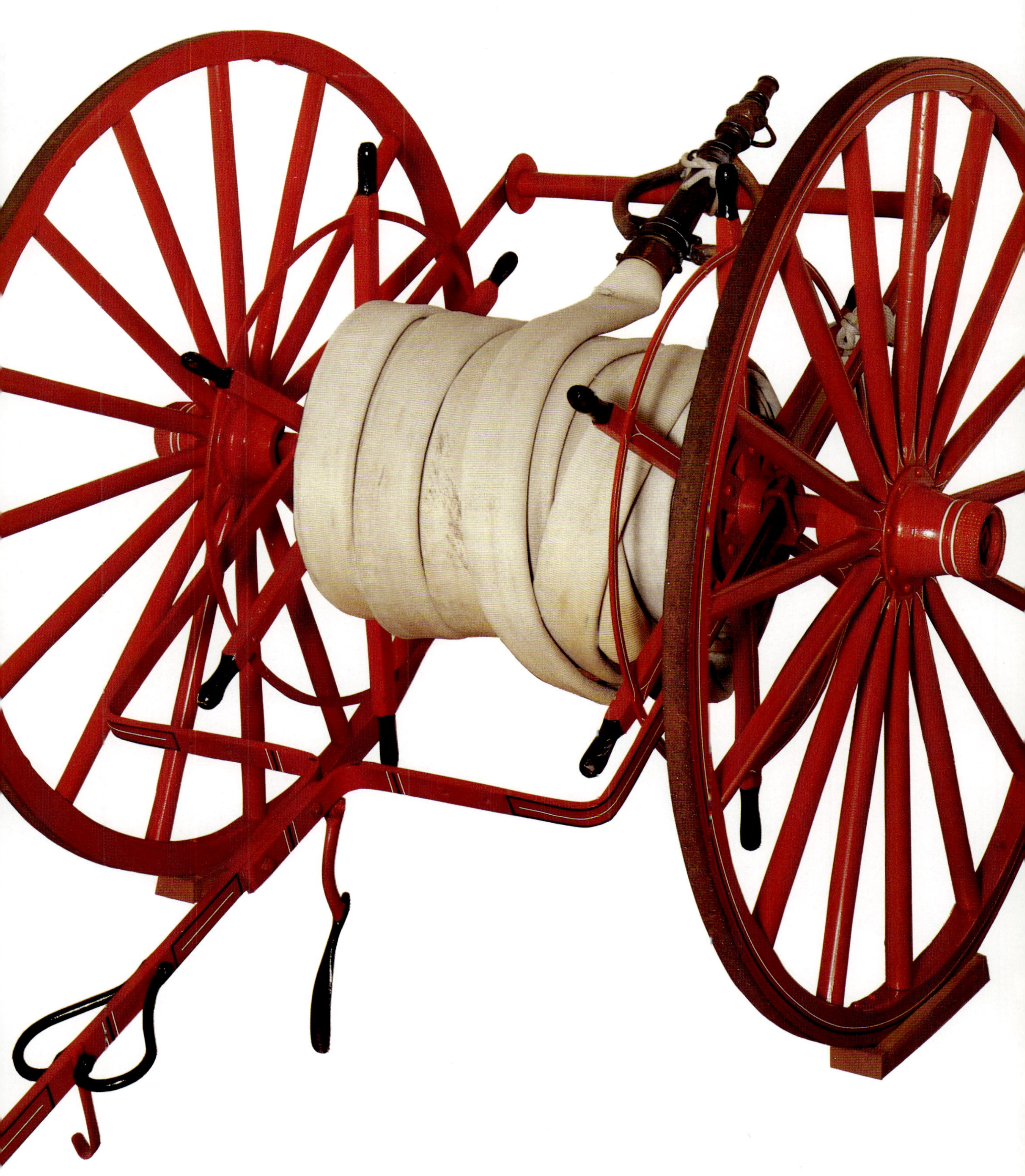

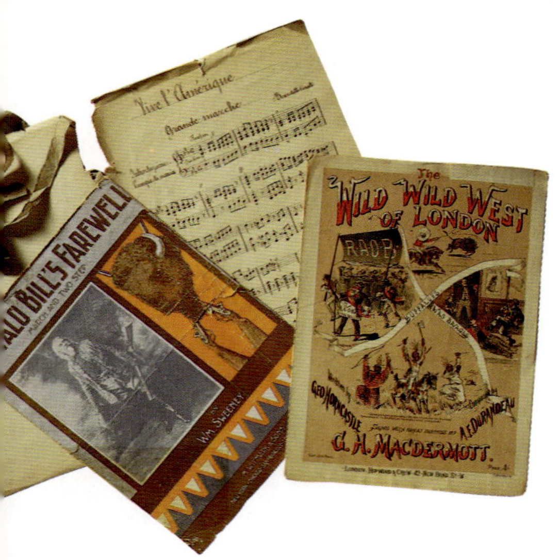

Left:
Sheet Music.
Music was equally important in the Wild West show and in early Western communities. During Buffalo Bill's lifetime, and after, numerous pieces were written in his honor.

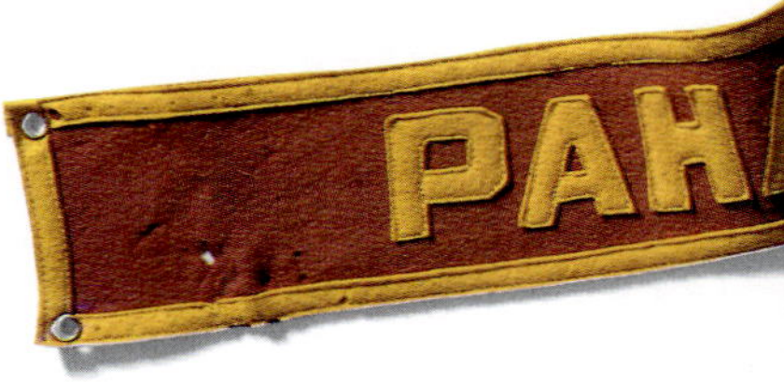

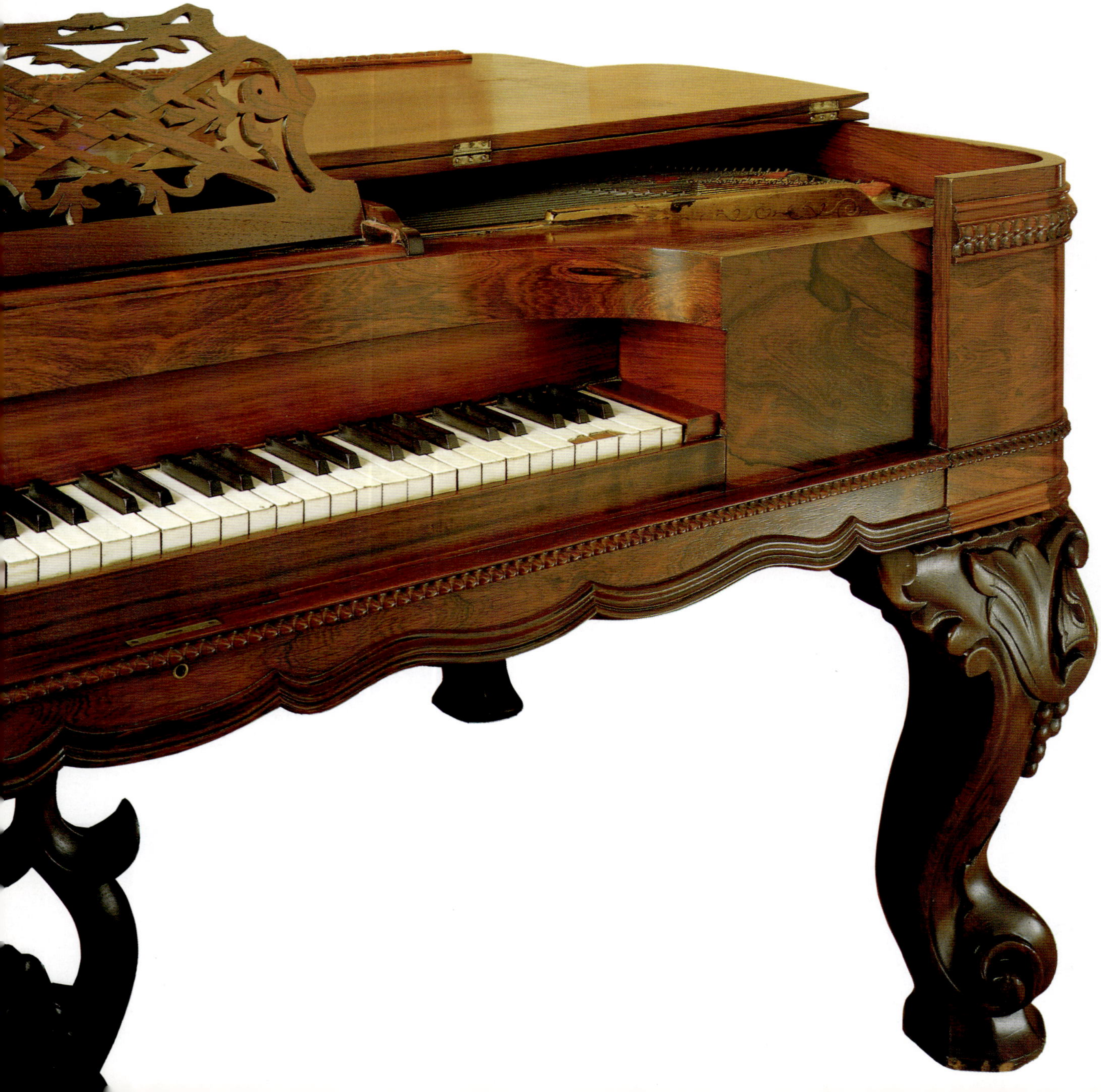

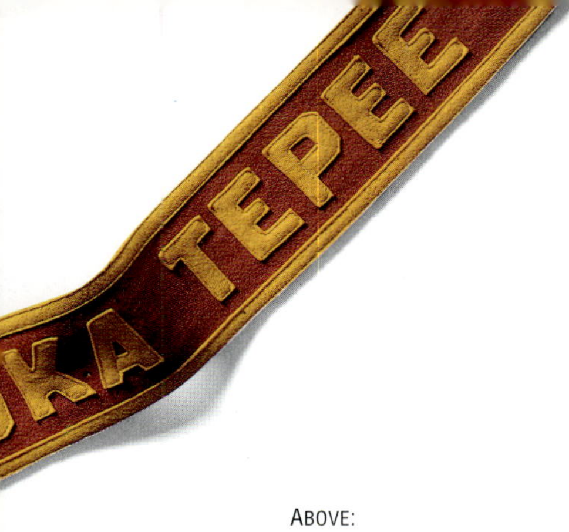

ABOVE:
PAHASKA TEPEE BANNER, C. 1915.

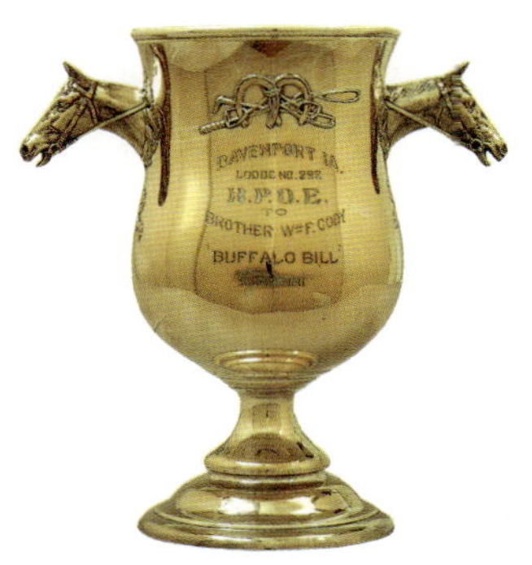

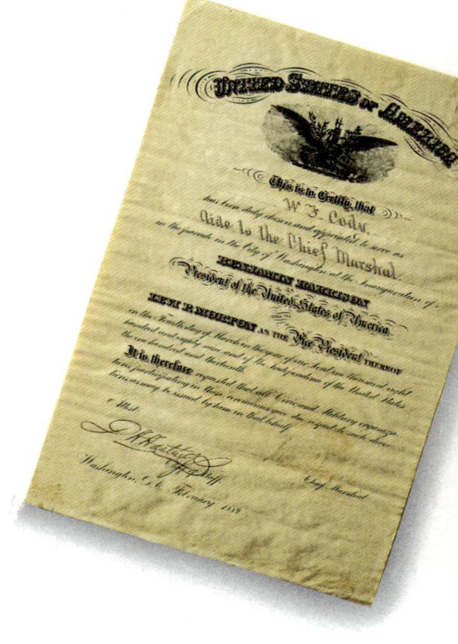

ABOVE CENTER:
ELKS CLUB TROPHY, 1911.
Buffalo Bill belonged to several fraternal organizations, including the Masons and B.P.O.E. This trophy was presented to him by the Davenport, Iowa, chapter of the Elks Club on August 3, 1911. In the absence of effective government, such societies were important organizations for commercial and social self-regulation throughout the West.

Despite hard work, a Western town was often a raw assemblage of buildings hastily and even carelessly constructed. The one exception was usually its hotel, a necessary lure for tourists and railroad travelers. Most settlers viewed the often incongruously ornate building as a sign that their town would prosper

Perhaps the first indication of such prosperity was the planting of trees, often where no trees had ever grown. The building of a schoolhouse was another important sign of growth. Still, intellectual isolation was often overwhelming. Some towns organized literary societies or hosted debates, spelling bees, dances and lectures. Clubs and local chapters of organizations such as the Masons and Elks were established.

Yet, failure was not uncommon. Some towns succumbed to drought. Some were abandoned by the railroad line they had grown up to serve. Many towns, the products of short-term mining booms, withered when the mineral wealth played out or when it became clear that the nearest markets were too remote for profitable shipping of raw materials. These failures became the celebrated ghost towns of the West, monuments to the unfulfilled dreams of pioneers and prospectors.

Short-lived or not, Western towns often provided more social freedom than long-established Eastern cities. Colorful characters—lawmen such as Wild Bill Hickok, unconventional women such as Calamity Jane—populate the legends of many long-vanished streets. Still, teachers, merchants, journalists and entrepreneurs formed the backbone of most communities and were active boosters of their towns.

ABOVE:
PRESIDENTIAL
INAUGURAL CERTIFICATE, 1889.
In achieving a pinnacle of personal fame with his Wild West triumph in England in 1887, W.F. Cody also reflected glory on his home state of Nebraska, whose governor named him Colonel of the National Guard. Thus he was an obvious choice to represent Nebraska as aide to the Chief Marshal for Benjamin Harrison's inaugural parade.

LEFT:
PIANO, 1850.
H. WATERS & SON, NEW YORK.
Cody's pioneers eased their sense of isolation by importing fine furniture and musical instruments from the East. This piano was shipped to Red Lodge, Montana, and hauled by wagon to Cody in 1900 by the E. E. Dunn family.

BELOW:
MOLESWORTH CHAIR, C. 1955.
GIFT OF PAUL STOCK FOUNDATION.
The town of Cody became a center for Western design and craftsmanship. This chair was made by Thomas Molesworth's Shoshone Furniture Company.

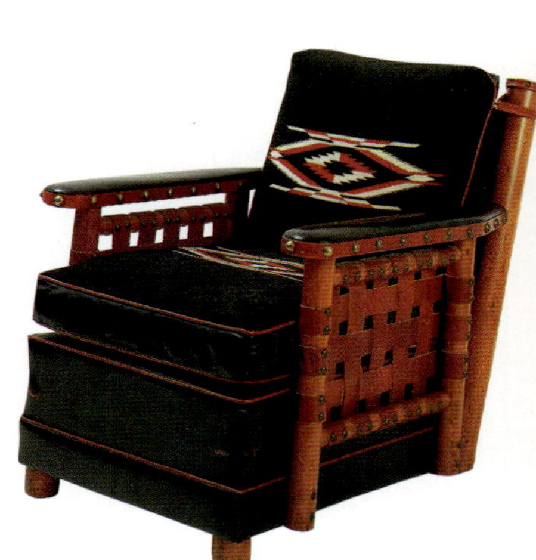

RIGHT:
MODEL 1895 WINCHESTER.
GIFT OF MRS. GEORGE W. T. BECK.
This rifle was a gift from Captain Jack Crawford to Buffalo Bill, who in turn replaced the escutcheon and gave the rifle to Cody pioneer George Beck.

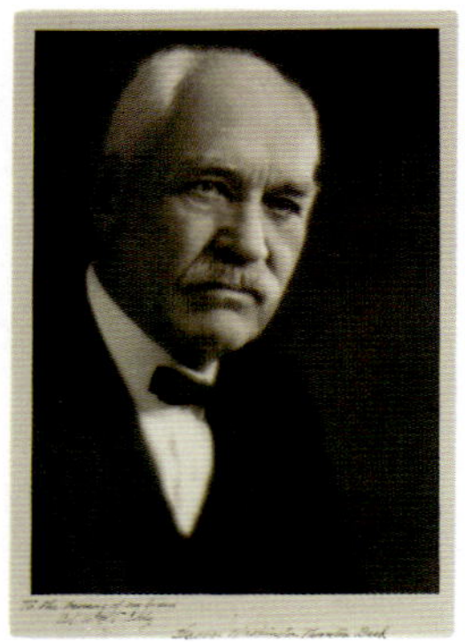

ABOVE:
GEORGE W. T. BECK.
ORIGINAL PHOTOGRAPH.
George Washington Thornton Beck (1856-1943), a collateral descendant of the first president, was born in Lexington, Kentucky, and later moved to Washington, D.C., when his father was elected to Congress. He joined the 1877 gold rush to Leadville, Colorado, pioneered sheep ranching in northern Wyoming, and managed the Big Horn Basin's Shoshone Land and Irrigation Company.

BELOW:
CONGRESSIONAL DESK,
OAK AND BRASS, C. 1856.
DOE HAZELTON & CO., BOSTON.
GIFT OF GEORGE W. T. BECK.
This desk was used by Kentucky Congressman and Reconstruction-era Senator James B. Beck. During the latter half of the 19th century, the future of the West and its people was shaped in large part through Congressional legislation.

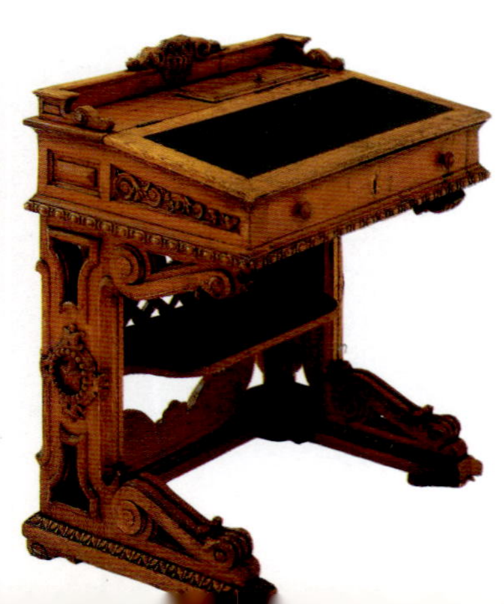

In many ways, the early history of Cody, Wyoming, founded in 1896, exemplifies the promises and challenges inherent in town-building. When George W.T. Beck decided to found a settlement in northwestern Wyoming, he recognized two vital facts: he needed capital and he needed water. Though the site he had chosen was arid and a good three-and-a-half day trip to the nearest railroad, it bordered a river and was close to some of the most spectacular scenery in America. With the right investment, particularly in irrigation, it seemed inevitable that the region should prosper.

Several wealthy developers joined Beck in forming the Shoshone Land and Irrigation Company. Among these backers were Nate Salsbury and Buffalo Bill Cody; the latter, it is estimated, invested over $200,000 in Cody in its first 18 months alone. Charles E. Hayden surveyed the Cody Canal in 1895 and laid out the townsite. By 1901, the Chicago, Burlington, and Quincy had arrived; by 1902, Buffalo Bill's Irma Hotel stood elegantly amid dust and assorted shops; and, in 1905, Beck founded the first electric plant.

But the town of Cody represented more than economic success for its founders. Like many settlements of its kind, it attracted a variety of characters who gave it a unique atmosphere. Iconoclasts like Caroline Lockhart and Sibyl Wilson were lively, often contentious voices in the community. Craftsmen such as taxidermist Will Richard, saddler Dave Shelley and furniture designer Thomas Molesworth provided skill and industry. And artists such as the regionally-known painter Ed Grigware and nationally-acclaimed photographer Charles Belden, whose Pitchfork Ranch spreads south of Cody, brought the town into the mainstream of national life.

BELOW RIGHT:
RECEIPT STUB, ENVELOPE, AND
CANCELLED CHECK,
FIRST NATIONAL BANK OF CODY.
SIGNED BY LOUISA AND
WILLIAM F. CODY, MARCH 30, 1914.
Fortunately for her family's well-being, Louisa Cody was not content to leave financial management to her husband. She was a full partner in their personal business affairs.

FAR RIGHT:
CODY, WYOMING, 1899.
ORIGINAL PHOTOGRAPH.

Throughout most of the West, towns preceded other settlement. They functioned primarily as trade and transportation centers for miners, ranchers and railroad workers. Though viewed less romantically than other facets of pioneering, townbuilding took courage and foresight.

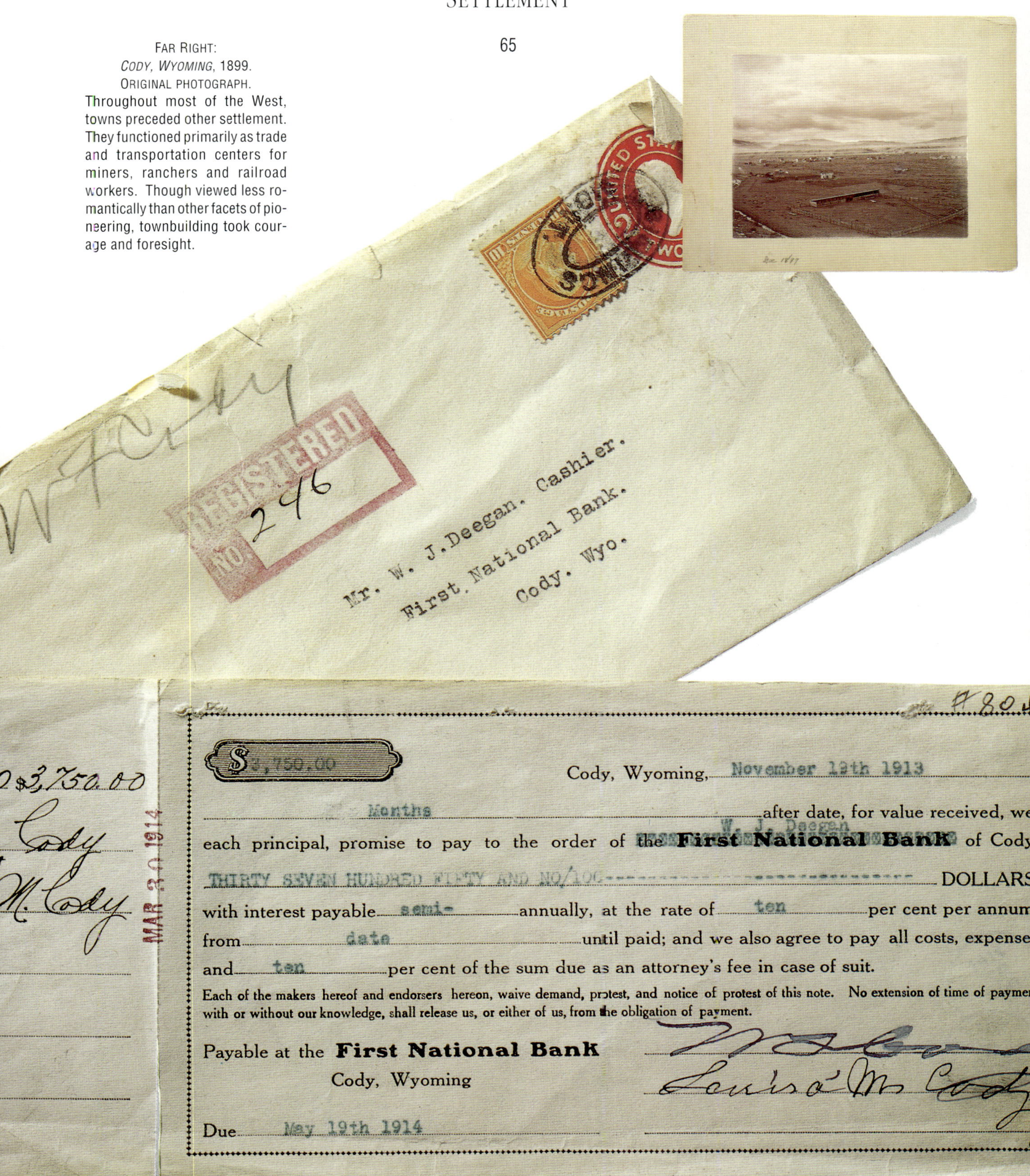

#804

$3,750.00 Cody, Wyoming, November 19th 1913

Months after date, for value received, we, each principal, promise to pay to the order of W. J. Deegan First National Bank of Cody, THIRTY SEVEN HUNDRED FIFTY AND NO/100 DOLLARS, with interest payable semi-annually, at the rate of ten per cent per annum, from date until paid; and we also agree to pay all costs, expenses and ten per cent of the sum due as an attorney's fee in case of suit.

Each of the makers hereof and endorsers hereon, waive demand, protest, and notice of protest of this note. No extension of time of payment with or without our knowledge, shall release us, or either of us, from the obligation of payment.

Payable at the **First National Bank**
Cody, Wyoming

Due May 19th 1914

Louisa M. Cody

MAR 30 1914

$3,750.00
Cody
M. Cody

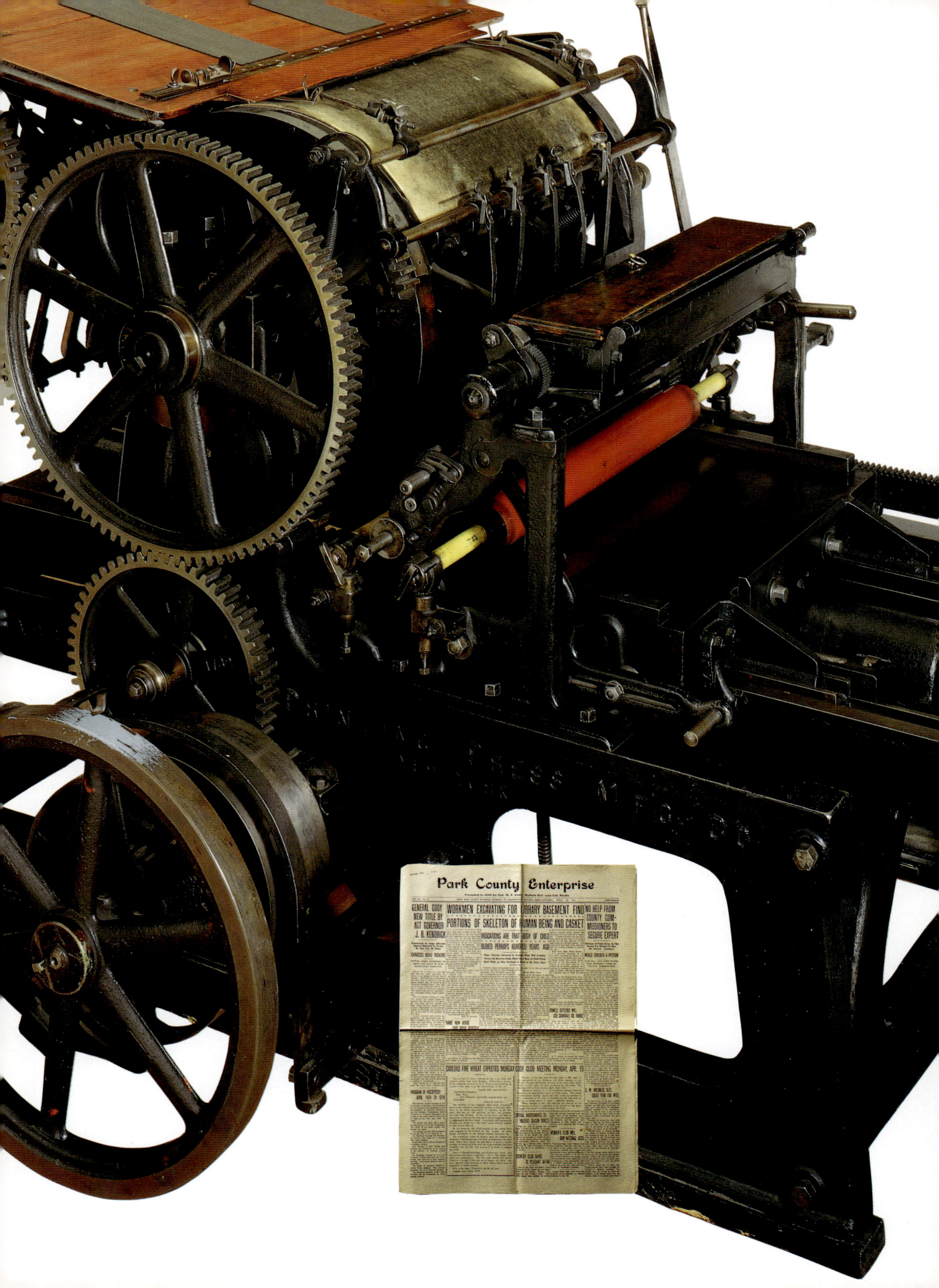
Park County Enterprise
GENERAL CODY NEW TITLE BY ACT GOVERNOR J. B. KENDRICK
WORKMEN EXCAVATING FOR LIBRARY BASEMENT FIND PORTIONS OF SKELETON OF HUMAN BEING AND CASKET
NO HELP FROM COUNTY COMMISSIONERS TO SECURE EXPERT
INDICATIONS ARE THAT BODY OF CHILD BURIED PERHAPS HUNDRED YEARS AGO
EXPRESSES GREAT PLEASURE
WOULD CONSIDER A PETITION
CARLOAD FINE WHEAT EXPECTED MONDAY
CODY CLUB MEETING MONDAY, APR. 19

LEFT:
BABCOCK DRUM CYLINDER PRINTING PRESS, 1899.
GIFT OF MR. AND MRS. GEORGE ABRAHAMSON, AND BRUCE KENNEDY.

Buffalo Bill purchased this printing press to establish *The Cody Enterprise.* Inspired by him to go west, journalist-novelist Caroline Lockhart became a controversial local figure. Strongly anti-prohibition and a bit of a crank, Lockhart owned the newspaper from 1919 until 1924.

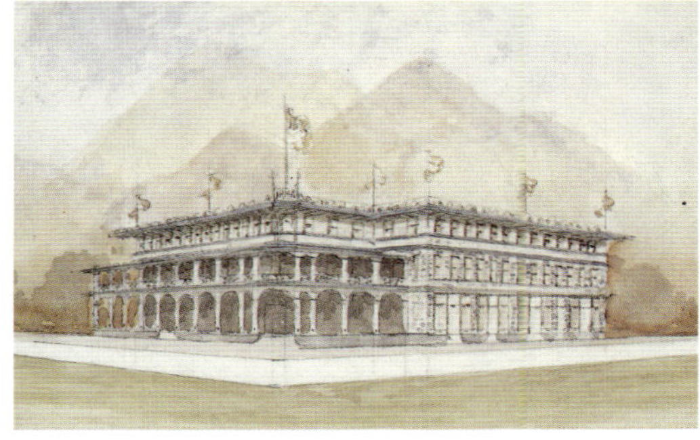

LEFT:
THE IRMA, ARCHITECT'S PROPOSAL, A.W. WOODS, LINCOLN, NEBRASKA, WATERCOLOR, 1901.

The Irma stood incongruously amid small businesses and shops. As tallied by journalist Charles Wayland Towne in 1902, Cody's population consisted of "44 broncos, 450 humans, three chained bears and a caged eagle."

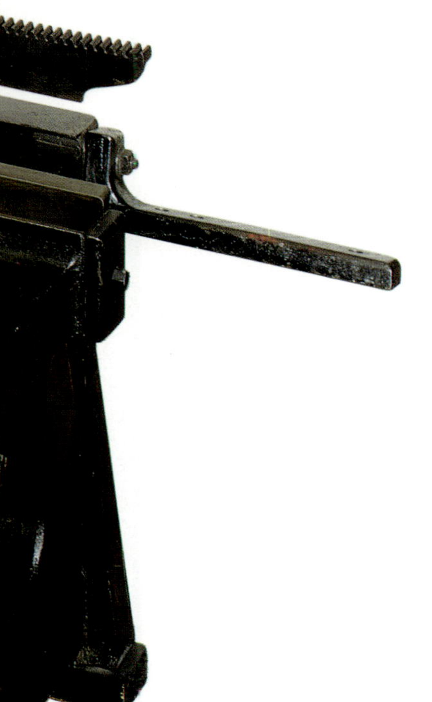

Many of the area's first homesteaders saw Cody's surroundings as a permanent home. Today, their descendants compose much of the regional population. Migrant laborers who come to work their irrigated sugar beet and barley fields every summer are reminders that racial diversity has always been part of the Western heritage.

Long ago, Buffalo Bill recognized and celebrated the inclusiveness of the American frontier. Though his vision has sometimes been distorted or watered down by subsequent generations, and though the West often symbolizes the contest between untamed nature and the ingenuity of white culture, Buffalo Bill's Wild West, like the real West it was based on, encompassed and empowered men and women from diverse backgrounds. Westerners represent many cultures and races, and continue the unfinished work begun in the Civil War of bringing unity and purpose to a diverse nation.

FAR LEFT BOTTOM:
PARK COUNTY ENTERPRISE, APRIL 10, 1915.

Originally founded as a mouthpiece for area boosters, *The Cody Enterprise* was briefly called *The Park County Enterprise* in honor of newly created Park County.

BELOW:
CODY (FROM LEFT TO RIGHT), 1899, 1901, 1904.

This series of photographs illustrates Cody's growth over five years, including housing for new residents, hotels, lumber yards, a newspaper and an electric light plant that was completed in 1904.

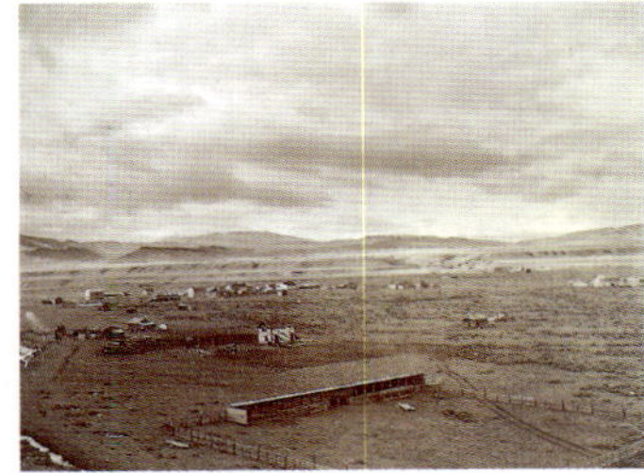

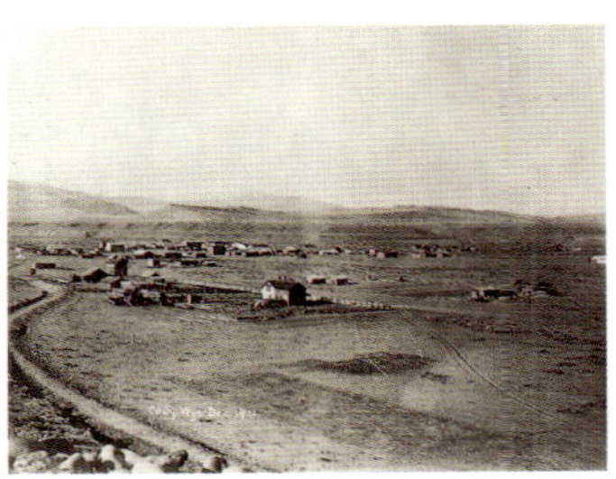

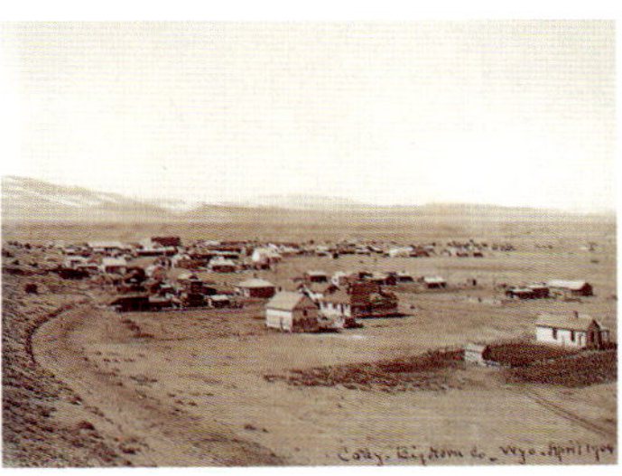

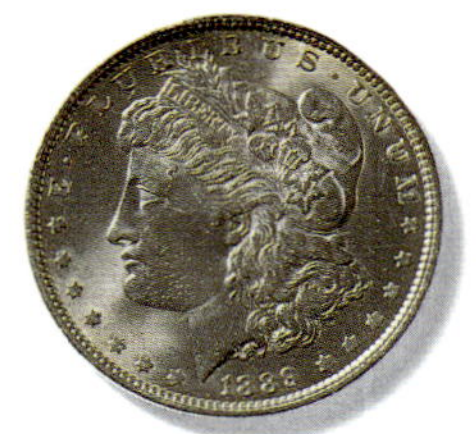

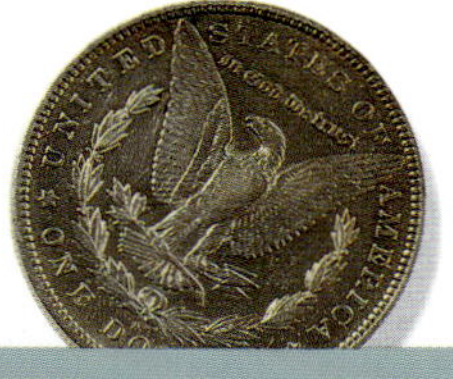

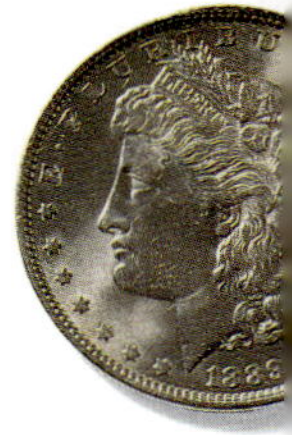

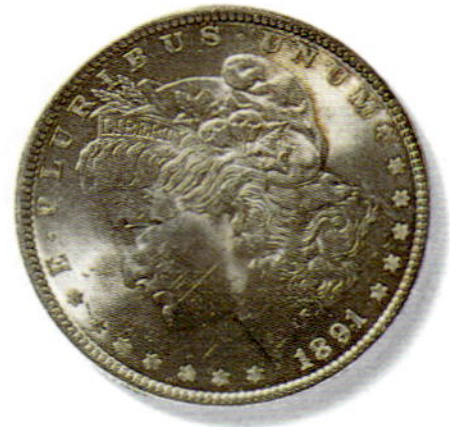

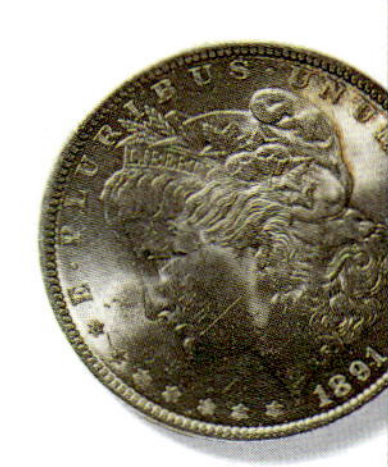

ABOVE:
COINS.
GIFT OF
ERNEST J. GOPPERT, SR., ESTATE.

WINNING OF THE WEST

There are many elements to the "Winning of the West." In Hollywood terms, it mostly means subjugating the Indian. It also refers to settling the land, clearing the forests, building towns and creating permanent governments.

The West is a land of sport and excitement. Hunters, fishermen, and tourists have crossed the plains and mountains for 150 years. It is also a land of raw materials—furs for the trapper, minerals for the miner, grass for the stockgrower, soil for the farmer and souls for the missionary.

There are dark as well as bright sides to the winning of the West. On one hand, some people see the West as a place where publicly-owned resources have been exploited for the private gain of a few. On the other hand, the West has been a land of opportunity for the many.

Depending on one's point of view, the role of government has been to referee competing claims to resources, or to encourage cooperation and make it possible for the individual to prosper.

People of all regions, races, national origin and social backgrounds participated in the winning of the West. It is an experience and a myth which has helped bind the nation together and define what it means to be an American.

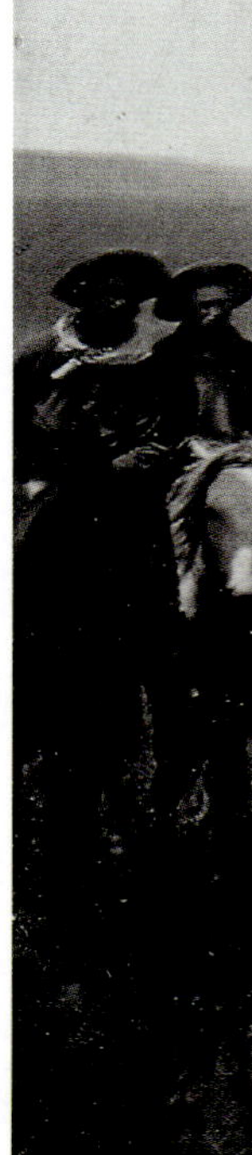

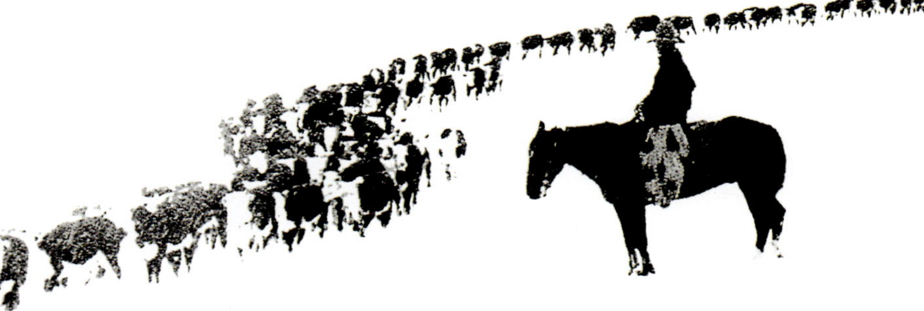

BELOW:
CHARLES J. BELDEN (1887-1966).
A LONG, LONG TRAIL A-WINDING–A HERD OF 1,500 CATTLE TRAILING ACROSS A BLIZZARD-SWEPT RANGE TO FEED AT RANCH HEADQUARTERS. DRIVING SNOW COMPLETELY BLOCKED OUT LANDSCAPE AND COVERED THE GROUND.
GLASS PLATE NEGATIVE;
4 X 5 IN.
CHARLES BELDEN COLLECTION.

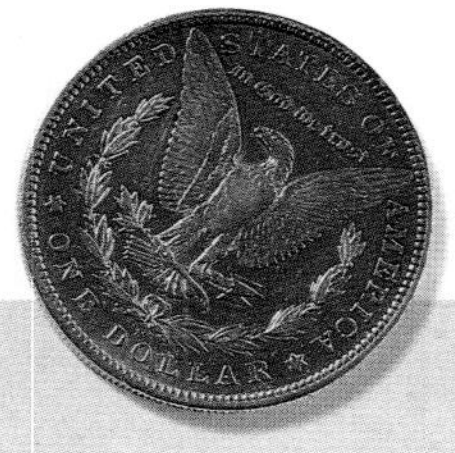

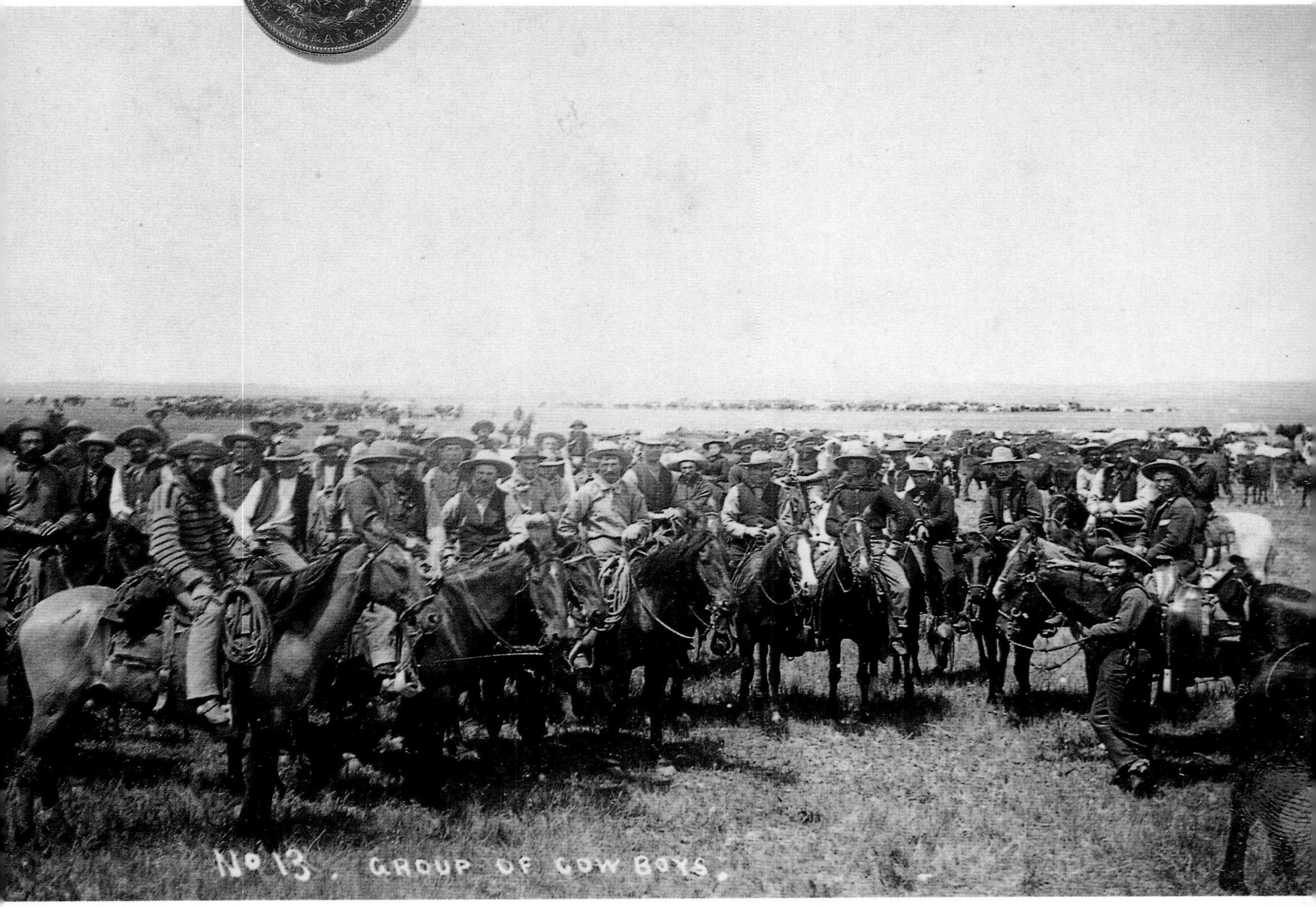

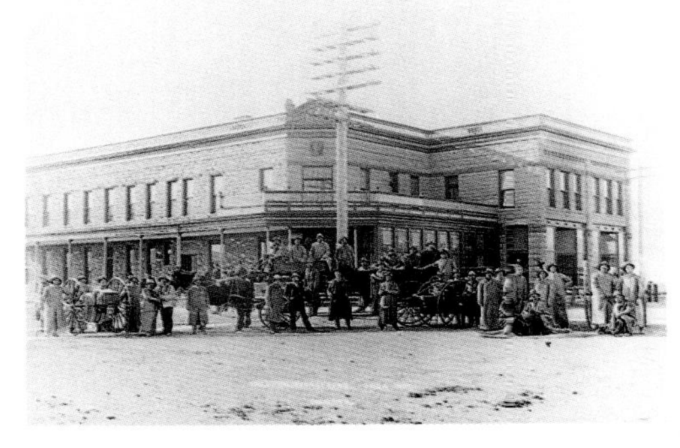

RIGHT:
BUFFALO BILL WITH THE
CODY FIRE DEPARTMENT,
BLACK AND WHITE PHOTOGRAPH;
$9^{15}/_{16}$ X 8 IN.

ABOVE:
C.D. KIRKLAND.
GROUP OF COWBOYS, C. 1880.
SEPIA-TONE PHOTOGRAPH;
$4^{3}/_{4}$ X $7^{7}/_{8}$ IN.

Board Of Trustees

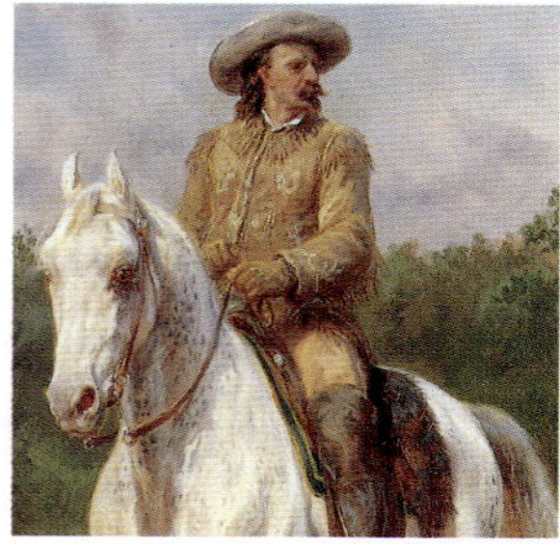

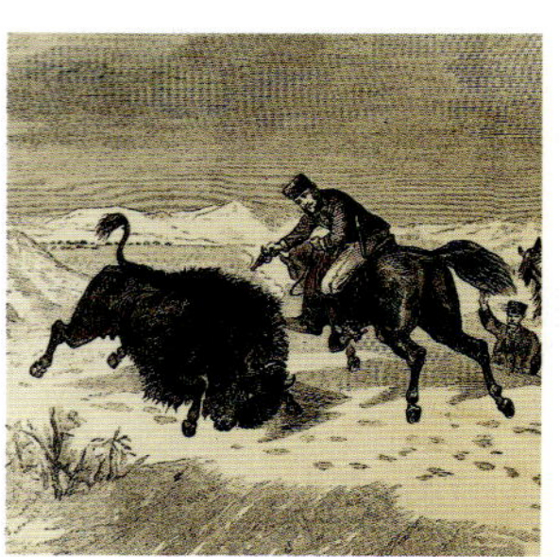

BUFFALO BILL MUSEUM

ADVISORY BOARD

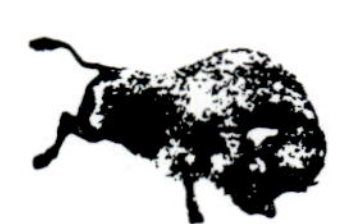

LIBRARY OF CONGRESS NUMBER
95-76822

INTERNATIONAL
STANDARD BOOK NUMBER
0-931618-57-6

PROJECT MANAGER
Suzanne G. Tyler

DESIGNER
Matt Hahn

PHOTOGRAPHY
Devendra Shrikhande
and Lucille Warters

Printed and bound
in Singapore by
Palace Press International.

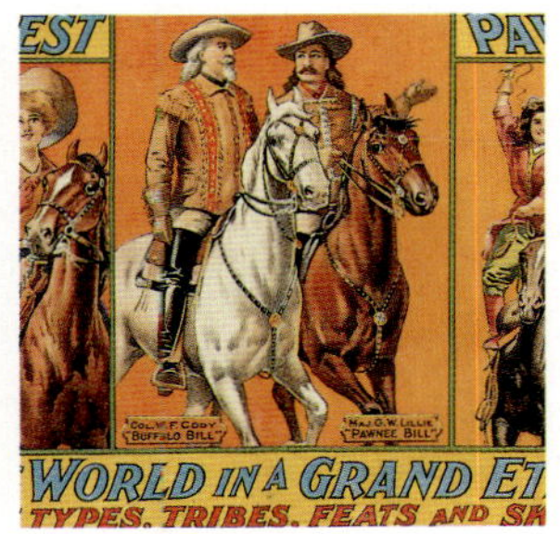

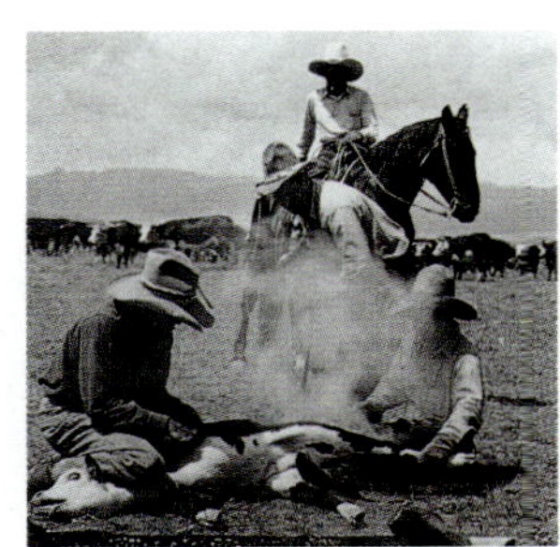

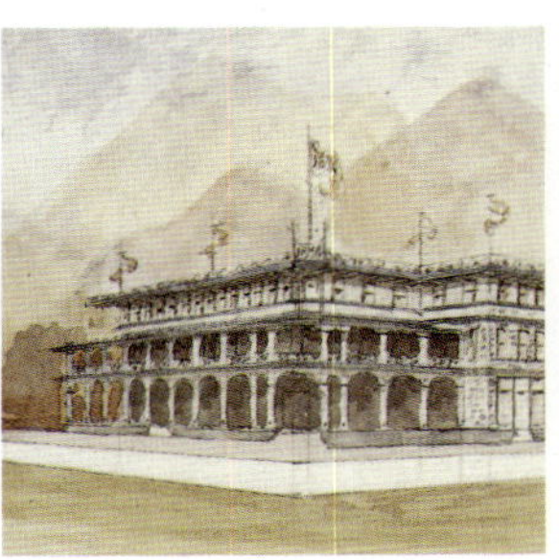

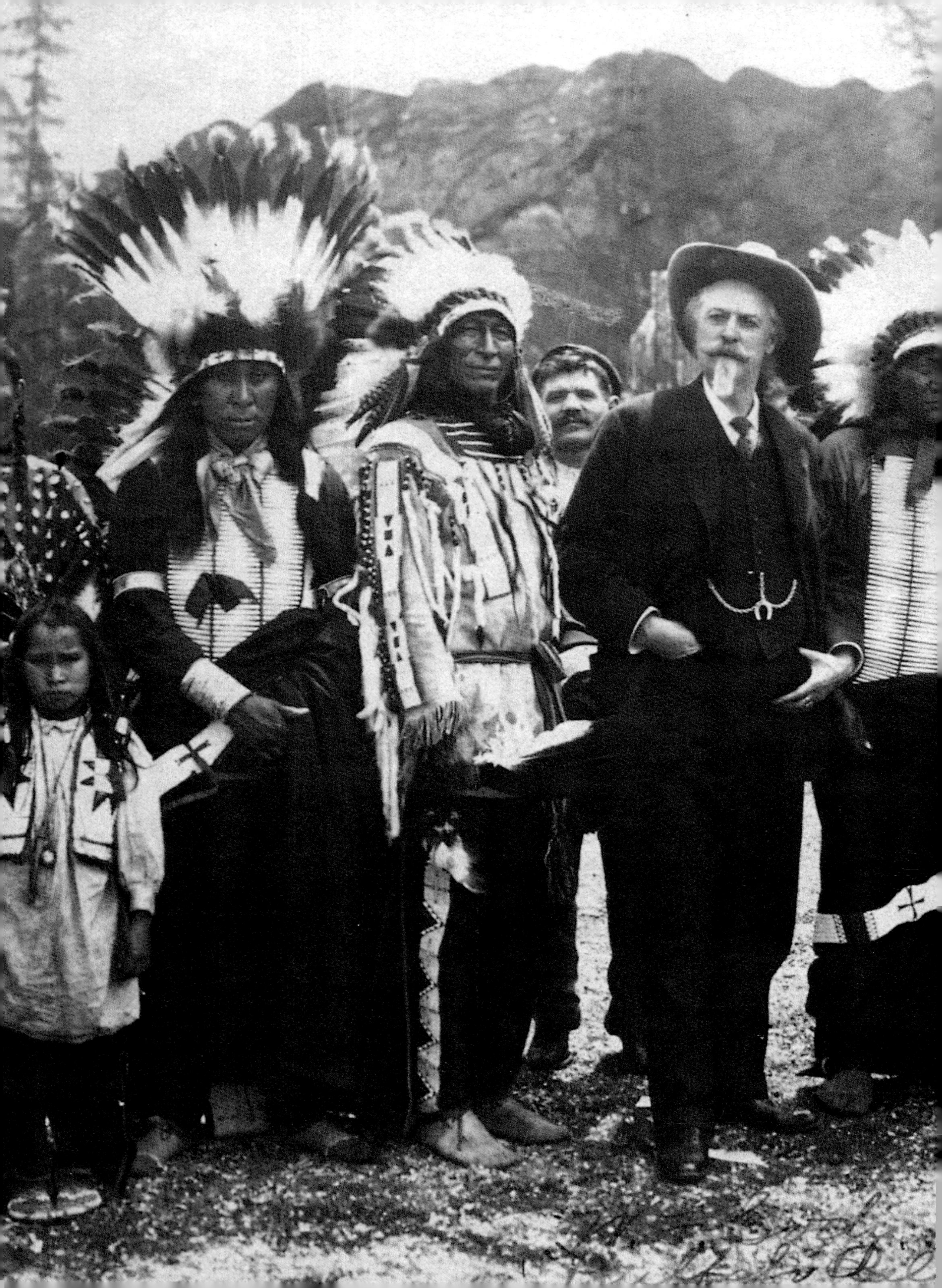